PLAY RESUMED

Some books by the same author:

Collected Poems 1948–1998
Telling Tales (Paradise Illustrated *and* A Faust Book)

*

Memoirs of a Mendicant Professor
The Alluring Problem: An Essay on Irony
Interplay: a Kind of Commonplace Book

*

The Oxford Book of Death
The Oxford Book of the Supernatural
The Oxford Book of Contemporary Verse 1945–1980

PLAY RESUMED

a journal

D. J. Enright

Oxford   New York
OXFORD UNIVERSITY PRESS
1999

Oxford University Press, Great Clarendon Street, Oxford OX2 6DP
Oxford New York
Athens Auckland Bangkok Bogotá Buenos Aires Calcutta
Cape Town Chennai Dar es Salaam Delhi Florence Hong Kong Istanbul
Karachi Kuala Lumpur Madrid Melbourne Mexico City Mumbai
Nairobi Paris São Paulo Singapore Taipei Tokyo Toronto Warsaw
and associated companies in Berlin Ibadan

Oxford is a registered trade mark of Oxford University Press

© D. J. Enright 1999

First published 1999

All rights reserved. No part of this publication may be reproduced,
stored in a retrieval system, or transmitted, in any form or by any means,
without the prior permission in writing of Oxford University Press.
Within the UK, exceptions are allowed in respect of any fair dealing for the
purpose of research or private study, or criticism or review, as permitted
under the Copyright, Designs and Patents Act 1988, or in the case of
reprographic reproduction in accordance with the terms of the licences
issued by the Copyright Licensing Agency. Enquiries concerning
reproduction outside these terms and in other countries should be
sent to the Rights Department, Oxford University Press,
at the address above

British Library Cataloguing in Publication Data
Data available

Library of Congress Cataloging-in-Publication Data
Enright, D. J. (Dennis Joseph), 1920–
Play resumed : a journal / D. J. Enright.
1. Enright, D. J. (Dennis Joseph), 1920– —Notebooks,
sketchbooks, etc. 2. Commonplace-books. I. Title.
PR6009.N6P57 1999 828'.91403—dc21
98–35295 CIP

ISBN 0–19–288108–6

1 3 5 7 9 10 8 6 4 2

Typeset by Graphicraft Limited, Hong Kong
Printed in Great Britain
on acid-free paper by
T. J. International Ltd.
Padstow Cornwall

Contents

Explanations   1

Excuse me, please   1

Playing around with computers — Huge means, small ends — 'He wrote it all with a feather' — The intellectual hunter — A collective, egoless supertext — Catching something nasty   2

Beaters and tracker dogs — Archimedes in his bath — In the end one has to do everything oneself   6

On custom and tradition — Dragged through the street and pushed off a cliff — Permanent drunkenness as a sign of good manners — Capable women   7

What happened to childhood? — 'Daddy, what's an alcove?' — A small boy mourns his father — The use of *Who's Who*   8

Outlandish proverbs — Better a snotty child — The loyalty of readers — 'Why an almanac, my dear?'   11

Men with qualities — New conceptions of genius — Sport as religion — 'Ooh Aah Cantona!'   14

Rich vocabularies — And constabularies — Queer Theory, Rend(er)ing Gender, and other strange proceedings in Chicago   16

Less is more — The usefulness of blurbs — 'The hour had not yet come'   19

Looking beyond the writings — Good writing as the
enemy of truth — 'This be the Worse' — An unlovely
thought   22

Grub Street and the vanity of human wishes — Large
hopes, little magazines — The arts industry — A joke
gone sour   24

Asserting one's rights — The coffee lady — How easy to
get things wrong   27

Personal column — 'Stand Corrected' and other fetishes,
learned and de luxe   29

The highest kind of teacher — Conditions for
understanding — And for misunderstanding   30

Why not be a writer? — Obsessive lust a speciality —
Modern publishers and their big cigars   31

The contortions of reviewers — Readers: an invisible
order of beings — Unpleasant, offensive, vile?: of course
it is — That grand word, freelance   34

A reason for not abusing children — The arts as trade —
Enlightened self-interest! — Nothing less obvious than
the obvious   36

Promises of paradise — Niceties and nastinesses — Sound
reasons for destroying books — Effects and side-effects —
'Ye shall be as gods'   38

The sorrows of the anthologist — And the shame   41

Mice and men: a story of Kafka's — 'Josephine will have
to help out a little' — A representative man —
A mysterious saying   42

A history of decay — Frivolity as a privilege and an art —
'Life belongs to dolts' — Once we trembled in caves; now
we tremble in skyscrapers   45

A man who had a worn-out nag — The foreignness of
foreign poetry — Is the fallacy truly pathetic?   48

Guilt by association — An author, despite himself —
The biographer as hero — Ill-considered texts   51

Old questions — The pros and cons of castles —
Ruskin's relations with the Bible — A moral tale   53

'God is no saint' — Being in the right all alone —
Is humanism namby-pamby?   56

Seriously significant, but is it art? — Make it news —
Frontears, idle tears — Accidental popularity — A line may
take us hours — Thinking and thanking: a semantic field   58

The old school — Hadn't they heard of toilet paper? —
Unholy pleasures   62

Real life: 'I live in a *ménage-à-trois*' — Economizing on
faith and cramming Sundays full   65

Humour, humid — No laughing matter — Three owls on
a chest of drawers   66

The art of the headline — 'Look on't again I dare not'   67

Women and the whip hand — A testosterone tax —
The key to Lear — Patriarchal punctuation — Grey areas   68

Dealing with foreigners — Who stole the mother tongue?
— A warning against heartless judgements — Old colonial
postcards   71

Advertisements and 'magnificence of promises' —
A champagne reception — The best washing-up liquid —
A fantastic hormone   76

Son of Man — For whom is religion meant? — Shoppers
and worshippers — A vacancy in the Trinity — A trade
union for the clergy?   77

Mind and body: who's master? — A dangerous and
infectious monosyllable — Donne goes too far   79

God as last resort — And as metaphor — An act of God
— 'I want to go to heaven to be with Sophie' — *Veni,
Creator!*   82

'Why should they bother what I say?' — Meeting
M. Lacan — A preoccupation with the incomprehensible   86

A free world — A smoking statue — Water shortage —
Selling soap: 'our sincere recommendation'   88

Sparing the Special Branch embarrassment — What
freedom means — 'I am not here to write' — Does Nature
go abroad?   90

Causes without effects? — Françoise and the formative
influence of reading — Who is Henry Cockton?   93

Should one read a book before reviewing it? — Making a
worthy sacrifice of vice to virtue — A film director saves
lives   94

Nature notes — The plight of male glow-worms —
Unheard love-songs — Not everything is meant to
be eaten   96

Recipes and restaurants — 'Remembrance of Tastes Past' — Artistic idolatry — Can Proust change your life?   97

'Rilke was a *jerk*' — Is it better to have loved and lost? — Unhappy consequence of studying Tennyson — Brains shrinking, skin growing thinner — To know more is to fear more   98

Why we dislike euphemisms — 'Safe S & M is like driving a car' — Wagner a substitute for pornography   100

Censorship, a filthy word — What Milton actually wrote — The road of excess — An unheroic couplet   102

Prose deserves the best — 'I look for a word' — How to pass the time between poems — Magic words that bring you riches   103

Killing charity — Tick the box — Keeping your strength up — How to make your will — The kindness of strangers   106

The word 'literary' may be troubling us — 'Our books are good in bed' — A better than sex cookbook — 'Incubus' fails to fit   109

The author, dead and alive — Standing up for literature — Emily Dickinson's bird — Confucius on the matter of language — Cod pieces in the supermarket   111

'Only the brute really gets it up' — Bookish lovemaking — Will the young heroine be raped or murdered? — Realism, roses and perfume — Safe sex!   114

Irony: what can be said for it? — 'Let them sing, as long as they pay' — A warning in a dream   117

Howlers, heart-warming and heart-breaking — The British government a limited mockery — A huge anti-semantic movement in Berlin   119

Is this what postmodern means? — Parrots and poets — Beware of laughter — Singing the Lord's song in a strange land   120

Caught in the Internet — Prometheus and Pandora — Are 'cookies' good or bad? Taming technology   123

Presentation copies — Finding something to do — The personal touch — And the impersonal   125

Working out the punishment — The moment Satan cannot find — Making the job last   126

Scene in a bookshop — Bibliographical musings — The price-tag — Books have their fates   128

Giving offence — Cap in hand — Bottom and ass — All babies are beautiful — Jesus alleged to love little children   130

Is it life? — 'It's *Coronation Street*!' — Or else *EastEnders*   132

Teaching and learning — Why Mr Eliot is important — Absence of mind after war — For but not about — 'In old age we all become mystics'   135

Languages, dying and living — Meaningful mistakes — 'Dangers and fears by way of supper' — Persecution by printers — Shackled by wordly desires   137

Life is not a television aerial! — Life is . . .   141

A counter-statement to Babel — Translators as busy
pimps — Do the French ever take French leave? —
The bandaged midwife and other mysteries — Translators
compared to casual labourers and waiters   142

A happy return — Closing an ancient file — 'What will
come after men?' — Seduced by law and order   146

Mammon, a busy god — A numerate society —
The glorious objectivity of money — Clearly it has
something to do with life   149

Not a swindle, but a behavioural issue — Other people's
money well spent — Cocooned in academia   152

Heavenly stories, no earthly meaning — The unfortunate
fig tree — How to shoot birds — War isn't like that —
A popular class of fable   153

Short c.v. of a spy — Meeting a communist in the gents   158

Obituary of a Chinese poet — The caring reader takes
care of himself — The advantages of inscrutability —
An exquisite sense of courtesy   159

Educating oneself against one's age — Epitaph on
academic philosophy — A season of German comedies —
A Jew quotes Luther   162

A deed at which the ibis and the crocodile trembled —
The ingenious unpleasantness of dreams — When
interpretation is not called for   165

Schopenhauer on a significant phenomenon — And on
beards — 'We sit and think, but do we sit and believe?' —
The meaning of punctuation marks   169

Having it both ways — Where to go for help — That
dread word, morality — A moral philosophy ought to be
inhabited   174

Making sense of things — The eternal verities —
The Matter of Britain — 'The horror of that moment'   176

Old people in the dock — The shirt of Nessus —
'How To Open' — What is nature trying to tell one? —
Charlus as role model   178

Sundry embarrassments — Putting oneself in the place of
others — Wrong numbers — The games words get up to
— 'Would you rather I painted a picture?'   181

A palm-of-the-hand story — What once was called the
water-closet — Bits and bobs — Farewell with your career
— 'They'll review this one for sure'   184

Modern instances — A virtuous housewife — Then we
can afford to die   186

A solipsist with barely an *ipse* — The Clinic is awash with
little bottles — We are sorry, we are too many —
A jellyfish on stilts — An existential illness   187

Good and bad: the proportions — Which particular end is
nigh? — It's always on the cards   190

The sentinel who knew Sophocles — Remaining in
uncertainties — The age of discretion — Death by
lightning — Ad libbing — 'Fly, if you love me!'   191

Carrying a stick — Where are your shoes? — Curriculum
mortis — A chilling little dream   195

Dogs and tricks — Does alopecia relieve grief? —
Criticism, for the young and hardy — 'Which trieth our
hearts' 196

Losses — Poets and their heavens — A literary estate 198

Index 201

PLAY RESUMED

A private journal, which is but a vehicle for meditation and reverie, beats about the bush as it pleases without being bound to make for any definite end. Conversation with self is a gradual process of thought-clearing. Hence all these synonyms, these waverings, these repetitions and returns upon oneself.

—Henri-Frédéric Amiel, *Journal*, 1877

If, as it is said, poets consider the passing phenomenon *sub specie aeternitatis*, then I am not a poet. I prefer to view the eternal ideas *sub specie temporis*.

—Francis Golffing, *Aphorisms*, 1967

As for my borrowings, see whether I have known how to choose what will enhance my drift. I get others to say what I cannot say so well, either because of the weakness of my language or because of the weakness of my mind . . . I would love to have a more perfect grasp of things, but I don't want to pay the high price exacted. My aim is to pass what life is left to me gently and unlaboriously. There is nothing I would cudgel my brains for, not even learning, however precious it may be.

—Michel de Montaigne, 'On Books', 1580

Difficile est saturam non scribere. But you had better try.

—Anonymous gloss on Juvenal

'PLAY': fairly obvious. 'Resumed': merely on account of *Interplay*, 1995, the first half, as one might lightly term it. (Which, let me hasten to say, doesn't have to be read first; or at all.)

Oh, and 'Journal': because it took many days, and refers to some of them.

❧

APOLOGIES are rarely out of place. Might as well get them in place straightaway.

To anyone misquoted or misrepresented here. Once I would comb the libraries had I the faintest doubt. Nowadays it's an effort to comb my hair.

To those reviewers and critics whose discernment and probity have gone unnoticed. To others, noticed but left unnamed. But for them, we might accidentally have read the books.

To the media. What would we do without them?

To competent and conscientious typesetters, wherever they may be. Where would we be without them? To others, who have made silk purses out of pigs' ears.

To the latest technology. Where would it be without us?

To charities that cover a multitude of sins and sufferings, are not puffed up, and do not behave themselves unseemly.

For being overtaken by events here and there: the penalty attending ephemerality. (Eternal verities, on the other hand, are covered by an enviable form of insurance.)

For havering and wavering. With his self-assured, God-assured rabbinical grandfather in mind, Dan Jacobson reflects on his 'own readiness to "see both sides of the question", the difficulty I sometimes have in standing my own ground, or even in knowing whether it is ground I stand on or merely intellectual quicksand' (*Heshel's Kingdom*). Yes, a feste Burg that God was.

For failing to offer apologies which might cause embarrassment, chiefly to me. Or because the grounds for them have slipped my mind.

Excusez-moi, s'il vous plaît. Sorry. '"Excuse me, please" – but for that apology, I wouldn't have perceived any offence. With all due respect, there's nothing untoward except the apology': Pascal.

> Do I repeat myself?
> Very well then I repeat myself
> (I am small, I contain one person).

❦

A WRITER friend tells me that at a dinner party recently he was so ill advised as to voice a dislike of computers. The other guests set about him quite virulently—as if he had impugned their sexuality or politics, or called for the compulsory repatriation of Asians, the return of capital punishment, or the introduction of censorship.

Why do people laugh superiorly at Sam Goldwyn's exclamation, as he brandished a copy of the *Complete Works of Shakespeare*? 'And to think he wrote it all with a feather!'

The computer gives one's writing a semblance of worth—more than the typewriter (a word originally denoting a lowly female employee) ever did—even of instant publication. One sees its charm.

'People are always trying to persuade me to give up my typewriter and adopt an Apple or a Mackintosh or a Toffee or something,' says

Jack Toledano in Gabriel Josipovici's *Moo Pak*. Then, they tell him, he will be able to play around with the words and the sentences. But he doesn't want to play around, he wants to move forward. Which was why he gave up writing by hand: he was too close to his own body, and the letters turned to doodles. 'With a typewriter you have to go forward, you have to keep typing, and that was the saving of me.'

But when the devil drives, one would resort to chisel, to spray-gun, to blunt pencil or bleary biro, even to a computer. So much of this is mere mystique, hardly less so than the debate over how —in which posture, in what surroundings—one should settle to read a particular book. Was Colette truly unable to read Michelet's *Histoire de France* when her father happened to have appropriated her favourite armchair or her special cat was absent on a spree? Was Henry Miller, who claimed that passages of *Ulysses* had to be read in the toilet to bring out their full flavour, forever on the run?

I could as well claim that the electric machine I am using these arthritic days spurs me on because it purrs like an exceptionally appreciative cat. We are not too surprised—though we may be foolishly disappointed—to discover that Toledano hasn't written a page of the book he was 'working on' for ten years. He has talked about it. For him the tongue was supreme, not the rather younger typewriter.

Technology grows ever more advanced and complex; we remain our simple and backward selves. A communication from the British Council, intended for a handful of recipients and requiring an answer of yes or no, gives an Internet site of twenty-eight letters and signs, and an e-mail address consisting of sixty-one letters, numerals and signs. The telephone, telex and fax numbers on the letterhead take up so much space that the date had to be overtyped and is barely decipherable. Huge means, small ends.

Or, as Karl Kraus put it long ago: 'Technology is a servant who makes so much noise cleaning up in the next room that his master cannot make music.'

From going to and fro in the earth, and from walking up and down in it, from making books and filling newspapers, from inventing the Internet, that he who runs may read and be as gods, knowing.

'How often must an enquiring man, an intellectual hunter, say despairingly to himself: "One man! Alas, only one man!" And he wishes he had a few hundred beaters and dedicated tracker dogs to send into the history of the human soul and round up the game. But again and again he learns how hard it is to find good beaters and dogs for all the things that arouse his curiosity; they lose their keenness of eye or of nose precisely when the true hunt begins. What one needs is enormous profundity, and overhead a broad heaven of brain power capable of looking down on a turmoil of multifarious experiences, surveying and ordering them and forcing them into formulas. But now . . .'

The above reads like promotional material: 'But now . . . we have the Internet.' It is a paraphrase of Nietzsche's musings on religion in *Beyond Good and Evil*, and the passage concludes: '. . . who could do one such service? And who has the time to wait for such improbable servants? In the end one has to do everything oneself if one is to know a few things oneself.'

New, new Grub Street. An American used to write long earnest articles on birds, trees, river-life and other natural phenomena. Now, more profitably, he works for CD-ROM companies, turning out bland para-length 'info-nuggets' on whatever topics the multimedia ask for. Bites at Eve's good-and-evil apple, hundred-word blurbs for books he will never write, building blocks, blocks of text which must have no manifest beginning or end since users will be dodging from one of them to another in no known order, 'net-working' as the brain is said to do in its 'intertextual' moments. These products of his must be exempt from 'voice' and 'attitude', those old tyrannies imposed by the erstwhile Author, for they would hinder them from melding smoothly with the products of his fellow workers.

The 'sexy' new technology—'sexy' suggests that intercopulation is at the heart of it—is championed, we hear, by 'wealthy software gurus' (it makes them wealthy) and by tenured professors of English (as communism redistributed property, so nonlinearity redistributes power to readers, or customers, by deposing the authors who provided the professors with their jobs in the first place).

The American, an ex-author now calling himself a hack, is in two minds: contributing to 'a collective, egoless supertext' brings in cold cash but no warm delight. He notes how speedily literary standards and professional allegiances can wither away in the presence of the new media's potent novelty and big budgets. Only a couple of years back none of his writer friends wanted anything to do with the digital revolution, and now a good half of them are into electronic publishing.

He concludes with the poignant thought that by 'the bleakest irony' he has participated in and precipitated his own obsolescence. So: Goodbye to you, and Hello, Mr Computer Chips. But can't we at least be spared the sound of intellectuals ironizing all the way to the bank? (See 'Virtual Grub Street', *Harper's Magazine*, June 1996.)

'Q. Do I really need to worry about getting a virus . . . ?
A. Your chances of getting a virus depend entirely on what you do . . . If all you do is play games and write letters, you have nothing to worry about.
Q. So what are the real dangers?
A. Viruses are little programs designed to be invisible until they start wrecking your system. Your best protection against a virus is never to use anything that does not come from a source that you know is safe.
Q. How do I know if I've got a virus?
A. You can buy specialist virus detectors with regular updates on the latest viruses out there, but these are only of use to people who are in a high-risk category.'

What does all this make you think of? Quite—but actually it comes from a newspaper's question-and-answer column, 'Dodgy downloads and shifty software can give your computer a serious infection'.

Someone writes to explain that our recent phone conversation was abruptly cut off because a fox was entering. What a splendid picture that makes! On rereading, sad to say, the intruder turns into a fax.

After arcane allusions to e-mail and going on-line, my horoscope this week says: '. . . don't worry, you're not alone. Just because you are not up to date with new technology does not make you a less valuable human being.' That's a relief.

❧

'ONE man! Alas, only one man!' Nietzsche pictured the scholar as an intellectual hunter longing for hundreds of beaters and tracker dogs to round up ideas for him. In *The View from the Bridge*, Pierre Ryckmans (also known as Simon Leys) observes that it is customary in universities (some universities) for senior academics to draw on the services of research assistants. As a sinologist, he must himself have qualified for such a privilege, but he never sought to avail himself of it—simply because he couldn't figure out how to make use of assistants in his research. If you could tell your assistant what to search for, you would already have found it. You can't send out beaters and dogs, bright young postgraduates though they may be. In reality you become aware of what you are looking for only when you stumble on it. 'Archimedes discovered the principle of specific weight while lying in his bath. Could he have instructed his assistant: "Go take a bath and bring me back the idea I am groping for"?'

Which echoes Nietzsche, himself a university professor who at most availed himself of the dubious privilege of sick-leave: 'In the end one has to do everything oneself.'

❧

IN an essay on custom and on not changing a received law easily, Montaigne tells of a man beating his father and observing that this was the family custom: his father had beaten his grandfather, his grandfather his great-grandfather, and (pointing to his son) the child would beat him when he came to his age. The father, as the son dragged and manhandled him through the street, ordered him to stop at a certain doorway, for he had hauled his father no further.

Traditions can indeed be difficult to break with. Alice Thomas Ellis recounts a story told her in Yorkshire by a cab driver from Kashmir. An old man had come to be a nuisance about the house, keeping the little grandson awake with his coughing at night, and so forth. So his son took him to the top of a cliff, from which, though it broke his heart for he loved his father, he was going to push him. First the old man laughed, then he cried. The son asked why he laughed. 'Because fifty years ago I pushed my own father off this cliff top.' And why did he cry? 'Because I love you, my son, and fifty years from now your son will push *you* off the top of this cliff.'

An ingenious appeal to traditional civility . . . A mandarin explains why he is permanently drunk. Of necessity he drinks with his superiors; he naturally drinks with his equals who deserve his company; and he drinks with his inferiors because he feels sorry for them.

New ways of dealing with old customs . . . The Chinese authorities propose to punish those caught burning paper money in honour of their ancestors on the grounds that the immemorial practice is not only superstitious but also a fire hazard.

But then, the Chinese have always been adept in adaptation, and briskly thorough when circumstances demand. Around 1920 the Christian warlord, Feng Yuxiang, baptised his troops *en masse* with a fire-hose.

Ancient Chinese saying: 'No matter how capable, a woman cannot make a meal without food.' Adopted and adapted by Mao: 'Capable women can make a meal without food.' (Jung Chang, *Wild Swans*.)

❧

CHILDHOOD is becoming shorter and shorter; soon it will last a couple of weekends.

When I was a child we lived in a small flat adjoining that of two elderly and refined maiden ladies, sisters who had come down in the world, Catholics I seem to recall. My sister and I grew very attached to the Misses Bruton, apparitions from a different class, as exotic as was the whiff of lavender-water that hung about their well-worn, well-washed, long black skirts. We weren't to pester them, our parents said; we knew enough not to. They were fond of us; we were exotics to them, I dare say. We knew them both as 'Auntie Bunting', the name Bruton being too hard or strange for us. And so it went on, questions never asked, never thought of, for a number of years, until the two Aunties died, or our father did.

Our granddaughter, Claire, called me Panda, her approximation to Grandpa. But soon after her third birthday, when I referred to myself as Panda, she drew herself up and said in a firm, no-nonsense voice: 'I *used* to call you Panda, but you are *really* Grandpa.' Childish things were already behind her. (She has now reverted to 'Panda', on the wholly adult grounds that I look like one: black circles under the eyes, a tendency to lurch. At times she adds, 'I called you Panda *before*', apparently rather pleased with her foresight.)

Out one day with Jamie, Claire's older brother, aged nine, my wife told him, 'We'll walk, you and I, towards North End Road.' (Being French, she's strict about grammar.) He mumbled, '. . . you and I, when the evening is spread out against the sky like a patient etherized upon a table'. Taken aback, she asked if he knew what 'etherized' meant. He hesitated: 'Something like asleep.' And did he know who wrote all that? No hesitation: 'T. S. Eliot.'

The author of an admonitory book entitled *Forbidden Knowledge* (1996) thinks it wise to affix a health warning: 'Parents and teachers should be aware that Chapter VII does not make appropriate reading for children and minors.' Chapter VII concerns the Marquis de Sade and the Moors murders, among other calamities. The only part of this closely reasoned book, ranging from the Fall of Man to the rise of genetic engineering, that children could possibly comprehend is the warning. Or so one would once have believed.

The TV critic, David Aaronovitch, tells us that when his seven-year-old son heard a bulletin from Washington which referred to 'oral sex in an alcove', the boy turned to him and asked, 'Daddy, what's an alcove?'

In some respects the condition of childhood is still observed. An eleven-year-old actress isn't allowed to watch a film she played in; she must wait four years. 'I'm sort of secretly pleased,' she says. She would prefer to go for an ice-cream with her mother, anyway. So would I.

'If I were asked to name the source of my poetry, I would have to answer: my childhood, which was a childhood of carols, Month of Mary devotions, vespers—and of the Protestant Bible, the only one then available': Czeslaw Milosz. Some Poles—even Poles—used to enjoy a measure of good fortune.

Is this a record? Our second granddaughter wins a prize a month or so before birth. A prize of £7.50 out of the hospital's petty cash or the nurses' pockets, as the most active, responsive and amusing competitor in her group of womb-age coevals. The nurses don't explain what they mean by 'amusing'; it would be churlish to enquire.

Children have a way of arriving swiftly at the heart of a matter; unlike their elders, who see richer career prospects in circumlocution and sophistry.

A five-year-old, toying with her parents' word processor, came up with this excursion into local history: 'THE FAMILY CENTRE'.

'In 1968 the family centre was ruled by a young concerler. His name was jamie. All jamie thought about was bi-mouthliys.' (Bi-monthlies? Wait and see.) 'The concerlers were sucking blood (you know what I mean). They were takeing money from the family centre. In 1969 the family centre was closed.' (Footnote 1, 'MEAN-ING WHY: The money was gone.') 'In the 1980s the family centre was opened again.' (Footnote 2, 'MEANING WHY: The money was back.')

Then: 'Little chirldren in the family centre/chirldren were noisy and happy.' But then: 'Time and close/it closed quickly after time and happieness.' (Reference to Footnote 1, 'MEANING WHY'.) 'But, then it was opened.' (Reference to Footnote 2, 'MEANING WHY'.)

At the bottom of the page, in bold-face, the verdict: 'The money comes and gos so we would not have to worry.' To be sure of the meaning there we need to hear the child's voice. Cheerful, resigned, cynical, indignant? Such a tale isn't likely to have a serene ending.

A press report of a more than usually ghastly killing, of a fifteen-year-old girl, peters out: 'When a murder like this happens it makes people even more'. Was the reporter struck dumb with horror, was it a case of aposiopesis, the rhetorical device indicating that strong emotion prevents the speaker from continuing? Probably not; there wasn't room on the page to finish, so many stories competing for space, no disrespect intended.

A small boy mourns his father, a police constable killed in Northern Ireland: 'I wish it hadn't happened to you, daddy, I wish it had happened to somebody else.' It had to happen, it had to happen to *somebody*. Such sad wisdom.

> *Now the good news*
>
> The young boy was given up for lost
> or at best for a vegetable.
> Happily his mother was a great reader,
> she had read about a cure in America
> (which of course cost a lot of money);
> and she read a fat book called *Who's Who*.
> Not everybody named in this book is rich,
> but all she asked of them was a pound,
> which even the poorer Who's could afford.
> So the boy flew off, and was cured, or
> at least much improved. Indeed he was said
> to be learning Japanese, which no vegetable
> has been known to do. This demonstrates
> the uses of mothers, the uses of reading,
> and even shows us the use of *Who's Who*.

❧

'IF gold knew what gold is, gold would get gold.' Who created all this popular wisdom? There were no soap operas in those days. To confine ourselves to George Herbert's collection, *Outlandish Proverbs* (i.e. foreign specimens), printed in 1640: some would appear to be the lucubrations of learned men. 'The words ending in *ique* do mock the physician (as hectique, paralitique, apoplectique, lethargique)' —that doesn't sound like *vox populi*. Born a few centuries later, this thinker would be concocting up-market advertising copy. And 'Critics are like brushers of noblemen's clothes' suggests an affronted upper-class author.

Then there are those, quite common, which could well be entries in an old *New Statesman* competition asking for invented 'Russian sayings'. Enigmatic, koan-like, surely meaningful, for they can't merely mean what they say. 'To a boiling pot flies come not'; 'One hand washeth another, and both the face'; 'Call me not an olive, till thou see me gathered.' 'Be not a baker, if your hand be of butter' and 'Who hath no head, needs no hat' are both undeniably true as far as they go, but presumably they go further. Likewise 'He that comes of a hen must scrape.' (Ambrose Bierce explained the term 'saw' by noting that, like the tool of that name, popular sayings make their way into a wooden head.) On the other hand, one can just about imagine a goose-girl jesting with her swain, 'If all fools wore white caps, we should seem a flock of geese', while the reflection, 'It is very hard to shave an egg', might arise in a poultry farmer faced with a new directive from Brussels.

'I gave the mouse a hole, and she is become my heir': this resonant, quasi-Biblical utterance, like some others here, is elucidated only by another saying: 'Let an ill man lie in thy straw, and he looks to be thy heir.' (A churlish version of 'Give him an inch, and he'll take a mile.') Similarly, 'It's a dangerous fire begins in the bed-straw' is, I imagine, kin to Solomon's counsel to his son on the subject of loose women: 'Can a man take fire in his bosom, and his clothes not be burned?' (The French proverb, 'La peur du gendarme est le commencement de la sagesse', must be a secularization of Solomon's 'The fear of the Lord is the beginning of knowledge.' Accordingly, 'It's a bold mouse'—but not a knowledgeable one—'that nestles in the cat's ear.')

Herbert's specimens occasionally strike a topical note: 'A white wall is the paper of a fool.' It is disconcerting to come on 'He wrongs not an old man that steals his supper from him', unless we assume that dietary do-gooding is at issue. A piece of advice we might feel disinclined to follow is 'He that would be well old, must be old betimes.'

'A woman and a glass are ever in danger.' Kindliness is not a favoured state of mind among proverb-makers, most of whom are plainly male.

'A ship and a woman are ever repairing'; 'When prayers are done, my Lady is ready' (intriguing, that). And marriage comes off badly: 'He that tells his wife news is but newly married.' Yet 'He that takes not up a pin, slights his wife' hints at some sharing of household chores. And there is one fine insight: 'The good mother says not, Will you?, but gives.' My favourite, robust literally and lucid figuratively, is 'Better a snotty child, than his nose wiped off', together with the tender promise of 'He that wipes the child's nose, kisseth the mother's cheek.' So that's why smart gentlemen always carry a silk handkerchief in their breast-pocket.

'Choose an author as you choose a friend.' An old compilation of anecdotes, for the most part edifying, reports that around 1750 the entire library of one of the Scilly Isles consisted of a bible and a copy of the History of Dr Faustus. (Presumably the English version of the *Historia von D. Johann Fausten* of 1587; 'A Discourse of the Most Famous Conjurer and Necromancer, wherein is declared many strange things that he himself hath seen and done in the earth and in the air . . .': blurb.) The latter had passed through so many eager hands that it was tattered and barely legible. A meeting of the leading citizens was called and a motion passed that a fresh supply of books should be ordered from Penzance as soon as the weather permitted. Further, it was decided that the supply should consist of another copy of the Faust book.

A heart-warming demonstration of the loyalty of readers. The following story, however, strikes a less happy chord. A professor at Saumur was so engrossed in his reading that he even missed his meals. 'I wish, my love,' said his wife, 'that I was a book.' 'Why so?' 'Because you would then be constant to me.' He would have no objection to that, said the professor, 'provided you were an almanac'. 'Why an almanac, my dear?' 'Because I should then have a new one every year.'

'THE time had already begun when it became a habit to speak of geniuses of the football-field or the boxing-ring... But just then it happened that Ulrich read somewhere—and it came like a breath of too early summer ripeness blown down the wind—the phrase "the racehorse of genius".' The urbane author of *The Man Without Qualities* (1930) went on to observe that footballers, boxers and horses had an advantage over great minds in that their achievements could be assessed plainly, objectively. 'In this way sport and functionalism have deservedly come into their own, displacing the out-of-date conceptions of genius and human greatness.'

Ulrich had thought he was doing pretty well in his career, that he wasn't too far from the pinnacle, but now he perceived that a horse had got there first. It came as more of a surprise than it would nowadays, when the term 'genius' is commonly reserved for those men and women who have won a couple of races, scored a number of goals (or prevented them) during the season, or knocked out another genius or two, when Norman Mailer acclaims Muhammad Ali as 'the prince of heaven', when we hear talk of a 'perfect' racehorse, and a football match is described in *The Times* as a 'passion play'. Which wasn't, though it might have been, a reference to the scourging of St Gascoigne or the crucifixion and subsequent transfiguration of the Blessed Cantona.

Eric Cantona has been described by another sports correspondent as 'a saint-in-waiting in the secular parish of sport' and identified with 'Parsifal, the holy fool'. (In a similar spirit, the ball with which England beat West Germany in the World Cup back in 1966, missing from men's eyes for thirty years, has been designated 'football's Holy Grail'.) It appears that, showing the selflessness of a saint, Cantona once prophesied that in time to come it would be said that Maradona was to football 'what Rimbaud was to poetry and Mozart to music'.

So figures in the arts are not altogether forgotten. We read that as a stylist the author of *Rabbit, Run* is 'a Pelé of the perfect word, a Maradona of the telling metaphor'. Happy Mr Updike!

Musil might have found a grain of comfort in one of George Herbert's 'outlandish proverbs': 'Gamesters and racehorses never last long.'

Ulrich's doctorate would have been in engineering, like that of Hans Castorp in *The Magic Mountain*. Engineering is an eminently reputable profession, useful, indeed necessary, betokening considerable intelligence, yet 'neutral', decently removed from the aesthetic, the literary. Mann's Aschenbach is a writer, his Leverkühn a composer, but authors don't always want their characters competing with them. They may prefer something malleable, disinterested, a holiday from themselves. Now we gather from the press that someone at Leicester University has embarked on a Ph.D. in 'Cantona Studies'. But then, Cantona is a man of letters, and has at least as much sociological significance as a boxer or a racehorse. And obviously more than Robert Musil and his incommodious ironies.

Latterly Cantona has appeared in the figure of Christ resurrected, on a large canvas painted by a Mancunian in Renaissance style, with fellow players grouped at his feet in the garb of Roman soldiers. The Manchester United manager, who features as Caesar, is no mean exegetist; he proposes that the Resurrection represents Cantona's triumph over his dark side after kicking a spectator in the stands. The Bishop of Manchester has given the picture his qualified blessing: 'This is a humorous painting which should be taken at face value.' Who's laughing?

And now Cantona is hanging up his boots. A sports correspondent mythologizes: 'He walked with his shoulder blades touching. He walked on to a football pitch as if he was doing the grass a favour.' (As far as we know, Jesus was rather more respectful towards the water he walked on.) A footballer's days are strictly numbered: not so those of a philosopher saint (short of crucifixion or some other form of violent death). Cantona had no choice but to be translated—the seal of his apotheosis—to a higher, if more rarefied, sphere. He has copyrighted his name and the invocation 'Ooh Aah Cantona'. Thou shalt not take the name of thy God in vain.

APROPOS of the word 'torrid', a character in Hilary Mantel's *A Change of Climate* reflects on our vocabulary and how it provides us with words we need and have never needed before. 'Words stacked away for us, neatly folded into our brain, and there for our use like a bride's lifetime supply of linen, or a ducal trove of monogrammed china.' She adds, 'Death will overtake us before a fraction of those words are used.' A sad thought; but not altogether.

After representations by a Cambridge bookseller in 1926 to be allowed to import a copy of *Ulysses*, the Chief Constable of Cambridge informed the Home Office that a Dr Leavis, believed to be a Lecturer in the English Faculty, desired the book in connection with a course on 'criticicism'. 'Criticism' was never quite the right word for what Leavis was doing (and some few people still do). 'You're always going on at me,' a wife complains to a husband, or vice versa, 'I'm tired of your criticisms.' Perhaps 'criticicism' is a slight improvement.

Subsequently, Ian MacKillop reports in *F. R. Leavis: A Life in Criticism*, the Director of Public Prosecutions wrote to the Vice-Chancellor in menacing tones, declaring that he did 'not pretend to be a critic of what is, as I suppose, literature, but . . .' The word 'critic' had been crossed out and 'scrutineer' written above it. Perhaps the DPP had doubts too. It would be nice to think that this was where Leavis found the name for his quarterly review, founded six years later.

The programme of the 1995 Modern Language Association's convention in Chicago, the great academic market-place, makes one wonder what one did in one's own professional life. How remarkably ignorant one contrived to remain!

A session on Milton features a paper intriguingly entitled 'Rough Trade: Milton as Ajax in "The Place of Punishment"'. Under 'Defining Bodies' comes 'Your Uterus Is the Loneliness in My Soul', apparently unrelated to 'If Wombs Had Windows: Pregnancy and Ultrasonic Discipline' elsewhere in the programme. A session is devoted to 'Henry James and Queer Theory', with one paper bearing the title — boldly plucked from that trousseau of words — 'Erotophobia'. Under 'Queer Issues' (a prodigious growth area) we come on 'From Translator to Transvestite: The Foreign Language Classroom as a Queer Space', 'The Queerness That Is Not One: What to Do with Women in Latin American Studies', and 'Gay Paree; or, Thank Heaven for Little Girls'. These objects of desire reappear under 'Hawthorne and Transgressive Sexuality' in a paper called 'Hawthorne and Humbert: or, Thank Heaven for Little Girls'. In current parlance 'transgressive' is washed clean of any judgemental tinge, but it looks as if Hawthorne can't be quite the man we thought him; another session promises a consideration of 'Hawthorne and the Female Nude'. Interesting, that so many authors are still drawn from the canon while the manner of their treatment derives from contemporary fashion and fad.

Among the darker sessions of unsweet thought is 'Mutilated Signs and Speaking Bodies', presenting papers on 'Rend(er)ing Gender: Mutilated Men in *The Duchess of Malfi* and *The Changeling*', and 'The "Body of Proof": The Politics of the Enthymeme in Webster's *White Devil*'; while 'Cinema's Anal Compulsions' offers 'Cinematic Digestions: *The Silence of the Lambs* and *Pulp Fiction*', '*Pulp Fiction*: The Anxiety of Evacuation', and '*Rear Window*'s Glasshole'. Other titles perplex only if you aren't in the know: 'Toward the Third Wave: An Argument for "Red" Materialism within Feminism at the Fin de Siècle' and 'Queer Feminism, Body Politics, and the "End" of Praxis'; likewise, if less intimidating, 'Pidgins and Practices; or, Brother, Can You Paradigm?' But papers on 'The Sentimental Culture of the Internet: E-mail and Epistolary Etiquette' and 'A Poet, Novelist, and Scholar Tap Dancing among Trade Publishers' sound positively enticing.

There is some parallel here with the wilder speculations of the medieval schoolmen: How many angels can dance on the point of a needle?; or, more in tune with current argot, 'A Stitch in Time:

Rough Estimates in *Paradise Lost*'. Except that our day sees far more scholastics jostling for position and promotion, and the fear of excommunication or the stake no longer exerts a measure of restraint. On reconsideration, the proceedings of the MLA abet the craven thought that in certain spheres there is something undeniably blissful about ignorance.

O fret not after knowledge! Sometimes it is more smoothly come by.
   'Do you know there used to be people in France called "fourteeners" who made a living by going along to dinner parties where the number of guests was thirteen?'
   'Where do you find all these bits and pieces?'
   'Do you know, I think I saw that on the back of a matchbox in a pub in Grimsby. I've learned quite a lot in life from the back of matchboxes.' (Inspector Morse, in Colin Dexter's *Death is Now My Neighbour*.)

Hilary and Ruth Anna Putnam, in the *Times Literary Supplement*: 'Because William James writes in an elegant literary style, it has often been supposed that his thought must be shallow.' A common enough state of affairs. In 1827 Goethe asked, 'What must the English and the French think of the language of our philosophers, when we Germans don't understand them ourselves!' And we know that German philosophers are reckoned the deepest of all their kind.

I've only known in person one man who believed that Claudius was the true hero of the play and Hamlet the true villain. And he didn't believe it. But it got him published.

'THE composition of vast books is a laborious and impoverishing extravagance. To go on for five hundred pages developing an idea whose perfect oral exposition is possible in a few minutes! A better course of procedure is to pretend that these books already exist, and then to offer a résumé, a commentary.' A brilliant suggestion by Jorge Luis Borges. But will it catch on?

Have been sent a book insisting that the novel didn't begin in eighteenth-century middle-class England, as 'we' have been incorrectly taught or have idly supposed, but has a continuous history, starting in Greek and Latin, of some two thousand years. (Possibly 'we' did know of these ancient novels, albeit as 'romances', even though we may not have studied them all.) The book runs (runs?) to 600 large and closely set pages, and belongs to the class of which Henri-Frédéric Amiel observed that it was the work itself that was displayed rather than the results, and the consequent noise of mill-wheels sent the would-be reader to sleep.

Books used to be much shorter, and more to the point. Leavis's *Revaluation* consists of 280 pages, and his *New Bearings in English Poetry* of 238, in both cases handsomely spaced. How did it happen that length became a *sine qua non*, and the ability to send us to sleep a recommendation?

Once it was my duty to compose blurbs for new publications. These blurbs were considered very good, but quite unsuitable. They unravelled the plots of novels whose plots were tortuous in the extreme; they summed up the arguments and conclusions of arduous scholarly books. Not everyone likes to be unravelled or summed up, and the authors, while intimating that they had indeed found the ideal reader, registered polite though firm objection. None the less, these little efforts of mine, résumés Borges might have termed them, proved popular with the sales force, who were enabled to persuade hard-headed booksellers that they had read and digested and admired the products they were hawking—and if they had, so would many others.

Perhaps I am deceiving myself. Sylvia Townsend Warner records a busy morning: 'Posted Viking contract, amended Enright blurb, permission of copyright to N. Y., & a surprised acceptance to Michael Schmidt for my collected poems.' (*Diaries*, February 23, 1976. The blurb was for her *Kingdoms of Elfin*. How extensive the amending I don't recall.)

And a passage of past self-revelation has just come to mind. 'If he could write books, why couldn't he write a decent blurb? Because blurbs need to be better written than books.'

'It is not growing, like a tree, in bulk . . .'

When an author has withdrawn or held back parts of his work from publication, or leaves behind him unused drafts, it's generally best to let them lie. Take *The Man Without Qualities*, a work whose size is such that to add to it seems an act of supererogation. On the strength of the novel, we know Robert Musil as enormously clever, yet light of touch, witty, ironic, wise, even disciplined, and (as writers go) unusually healthy. And thoroughly aware of the categories of writing, pretentious, kitschy, sensational, laboured, which he wouldn't be seen dead with—and which, were such a thing humanly possible, you would think he had himself killed off for good.

Now we are presented with some 700 pages of 'posthumous papers', ranging from whole chapters discarded at galley stage to brief passages which one fine day might or might not have been inserted somewhere in the novel. Some of the material is *echt* or reasonably *echt* Musil—his mind was so rich, he couldn't easily spend all of it—but a surprising proportion falls into one or other of those never-to-be-condoned categories. Hardly the work of the same writer, you would say. It's as if the years spent on this unfinished and unfinishable novel had made a sick man of him. Though not sick enough to have authorized publication of these left-overs.

The haiku

>Gaspings and gulpings,
>Poetic equivalent
>Of emphysema —

>It has its assets:
>It scurries through the middle
>And lights on the end.

Borges tells a story about a Swedish thinker who pointed out that Judas's act was wholly superfluous since there was no need to identify a famous preacher, a figure so well known to his enemies. Therefore there had to be another reason for it. Namely, that when, to redeem the human race, God lowered himself to be a man, He made himself a man in all completeness, capable not only of weariness, confusion, thirst and pain, but also of sin—and of that most infamous of sins, the betrayal of a friend and master. God could have chosen to be Alexander or Socrates or Virgil or even the preacher Jesus, but He chose to be Judas.

Alas, the bookshops of Stockholm could not shift the volume in which the thinker expounded his thoughts. From this he gathered that God had commanded a vast indifference, for He did not wish his terrible secret to be revealed throughout the world. 'The hour had not yet come.'

When our books fail, we too tell ourselves that their hour has not yet come; but we rarely infer some divine interdiction—which could last heaven knows how long.

WHEN choosing a school for her son, Mary Shelley asked a friend for advice. The friend, somewhat at a loss, said, 'Oh, send him somewhere where they will teach him to think for himself.' Mrs Shelley replied, or is said to have replied, 'Oh, my God, teach him rather to think like other people!'

When one is urged to 'Know thyself', the retort bursts out, 'Oh, my God, rather let me know some other self, any other self!' Does the allure of biography lie here? But then it appears that other selves are not so very other. A little worse in one respect, it may be, a little better in another, usually more than a little cleverer. One goes on, oh, my God, knowing oneself.

A biographer's professed aim is 'to look beyond the writings and into the artist'. So the artist lies beyond the writings? No, the writings lie beyond the artist.

Another Life of Thomas Mann has come out. Which makes three of them in rapid succession. 'Perfection of the life, or of the work . . .' How could the author of *The Magic Mountain*, *Doctor Faustus*, *Felix Krull*, have much life to speak of—at any rate, to write about—outside those works? With such a vivid and varied inner life, what room for any very notable outer one?

Mann's funeral in Switzerland in 1955 was attended by important personages from both Germanies. The wreaths from the Democratic Republic featured hammers and sickles, and it was decided that they were too large to pass through the church doors and had better be left outside. Naturally this drew angry protests from the East Germans. The incident would have appealed to Mann's taste for simple comedy (less remarked on than his celebrated irony), but might have distressed him too. Politics oughtn't to raise its voice in the very porch. Couldn't a non-political man be allowed a non-political farewell?

But no doubt that question begs the question.

In his memoir, *Not Entitled*, Frank Kermode notes shrewdly that in autobiography the principal enemy of the truth is 'not mendacity but good writing'. The autobiographer, above all, wants to write well, in harmony with the subject rather than the truth. After all, it's the style that's the man. More generally, William Empson admitted that 'Checking references always seems to me a trivial duty compared to checking style.' And the polemicist Karl Kraus wasn't far off the point in his aphorism, 'I trim my opponents to fit my arrows.' There's no art without tarting up.

'If you turn over a Modern Master, you'll probably find a Modern Mistress': a smart-arse (for once understating things) in Malcolm Bradbury's *Doctor Criminale*.

Apropos of Philip Larkin and his posthumous fate, Robert Conquest sends me his verse, 'This be the Worse', which begins:

> They fuck you up, the chaps you choose
> To do your Letters and your Life.
> They wait till all that's left of you's
> A corpse in which to shove a knife.

According to a biography, the golden calf was four and a half inches high, four and a half inches long, and made of bronze.

My father was hot-tempered, volatile, improvident, a bit of a fantasist, good-looking, charming on occasion, popular with his workmates, and (though no drunkard) fond of a drink. (Which meant he was Irish, as we then saw it.) It's only now, advanced in years, that I find myself wondering about the times he went missing for a day or two, and no one could trace him or the post-office van he had driven into the wilds of Warwickshire. These disappearances usually happened around Christmas. Had the van really broken down in some sequestered spot? Had he been searching in the snow and the dark of evening for far-flung farms, to deliver cards and presents? (Our mother was very worried; so were we kids, we might not be getting any presents.) Or had he been up to no good with the milkmaids?

Why has this unlovely thought, unfilial and implausible, not to say un-Irish, struck me only now? Surely because of the biographies, or for the most part reviews of biographies, I have been reading of late.

If biography is a sin, it's advisable to heed that ancient counsel and hate the sin but love the sinner. Otherwise one will have no friends left.

❧

MORE about Grub Street, and the vanity of human wishes.

'In November 1727, in consequence of an Affray at Robinson's Coffeehouse, Charing Cross, he was arrested on a capital charge of Wounding and Murder, found guilty by a Grand Jury Court at the Old Bailey, and condemned to suffer execution at Tyburn.' Thanks to the intercession of several influential personages, possibly including Queen Caroline, he received a royal pardon. 'He immediately thereafter tasted the delights of Celebrity, and applied precipitously for the position of Poet Laureate; which, failing to obtain, he appointed himself "Volunteer Laureate" to the Queen, thereby obtaining an Allowance of £50 per annum until her majesty's death in 1737.' The Queen's allowance having ceased, 'he was thrown once more upon his Wits and his Friends', though it is to be feared that he often passed his nights 'in the Cellars and on the Bulks of Covent Garden, in the company of Beggars, Thieves, and other Denizens of Grub Street'. (From an obituary of Mr Richard Savage, Gent., composed by Richard Holmes in 1993.) It wouldn't happen these days, not quite in that way.

'In January 1743 he was precipitately arrested for Debt, and conveyed to the Newgate Prison in Bristol, where he received the personal Attentions of the Gaoler Mr Dagg, and died suddenly in his

Room on 1st August 1743.' That's more likely, given a prison governor half as humane and solicitous as Mr Dagg—of which 'tender gaoler', Dr Johnson observed memorably that 'Virtue is undoubtedly most laudable in that state which makes it most difficult.'

The delights of celebrity . . . It won't do, just sitting quietly at home bent over a cold computer or rackety typewriter. Concerning the sudden demand for the work of Richard Savage, Henry Fielding remarked that henceforth publishers took care 'to provide themselves with such writers as were in the fairest way of being hanged'.

'How about we all sit down and knock together a journal or a commonplace book or an anthology, something like that, or do a spot of reviewing for a bob or two? It's all the rage these days.' See Schiller's play of 1780, *The Robbers*: a gang of malcontents in a tavern, discussing ways of making a living.

Little magazines, it is commonly said, are where writers find their beginnings. Little magazines are also where—after having stopped over at such notable locations as the *Sunday Times*, *Observer*, *New York Review of Books*, *London Review of Books*—they tend to find their ends. There is a little magazine in Martin Amis's *The Information* (a book well calculated to turn the starriest-eyed young hopeful off the literary life), which is called *The Little Magazine*. 'It really did stand for something, in this briskly materialistic age. It stood for not paying people.'

A publisher asks for my next, very short book to be delivered on disk. My agent asks, do I have a computer? No, but I have a typewriter. Do they want me to bind the book, too? She doesn't seem too sure.
  If the advance were in the vicinity of £500,000 or even £10,000 I'd print and peddle it for them. As it is, they will charge me £75 for transferring the typescript to disk. Mercifully, this sum is to be deducted from royalties after the £400 advance has been earned.

> They tell me that my works
> Will have to be transposed
> From sturdy stone to flimsy 'parchment'
> New fangled out of some old goat.
> It won't catch on, not ever —
> One might as well write on water.
>
> Next it seems there'll be a trick called 'rhyme'
> But not, most certainly not, in my time.

Further humiliation. At a party I am introduced to a young woman working for the Arts Council, Literature Department. 'We don't give you any money, do we?' she remarks, to get the conversation going. Fatally, I try to make a joke. 'There *is* something you could do for me.' Namely give me £120 to pay off permission fees incurred by a forthcoming book, 'literary' and hence unprofitable. 'We don't do that kind of thing,' the young woman says, as if it were an indecent proposal. 'We subsidize certain publishers, and of course we give money to young writers.' The adjective comes out in italics.

Nothing sours the temper more than a pleasantry gone wrong. I restrict myself to a scowl, and seek relief in telling the story to a couple of young reporters, no doubt agog for scandal. They shake their heads, they consider ageism quite deplorable. They turn out to be waiters.

George Walden on contemporary British art, the 'arts industry' ('a very twentieth-century solecism') and patronage: 'Artists go through the motions of biting the official hand that feeds them, and the State, rich collectors and the media go through the motions of wincing at the pain.' I assume it's in order to take a tiny bite at the hand that doesn't feed you?

'I do not like the crudity of the words "rich" and "poor".' Thus Lord Gowrie, Chairman of the Arts Council of England, apropos of £55 million granted to the Royal Opera House, Covent Garden, with a 'top-up' of a further £23 million to follow.

Quite a number of us don't like the crudity of those words.

Twelve months after editing a selection from a seventeenth-century poet for a paperback series, I am invited to embark on another poet, same length, same format. Could the fee be increased a little, I ask, if only in step with inflation? No, comes the stern and bracing answer: 'We do not recognize inflation here.' A couple of months later I am sent a proof of the book's cover, and see that the series price has gone up by 100 per cent.

Lurking here, I imagine, are those tell-tale market forces, the forces that really count, and so rarely count in one's favour.

If you pay peanuts, you'll get—the likes of me.

❦

AT Chatto we were always getting typescripts from would-be novelists and thinkers, no-hopers who hopefully inscribed the symbol © at the bottom of every single page. If wise in no other way, they were worldly-wise. (There were those, too, who had no typescript to offer but wrote to warn us that some author or other—not necessarily one of ours—had stolen their thoughts by means of brain-waves or mental rays and made a book of them. In 1748, soon after the publication of *Clarissa*, a woman wrote in high indignation to Samuel Richardson, who had, she asserted, made public the story of her own life, not a word of which she had ever told to anyone.) More surprising is the declaration, no doubt a sign of some aspect of the times, commonly seen on the copyright page of published books: 'The author has asserted his moral rights.' What does this mean? Is it general or specific? Is the author offering or demanding? Does it apply to pornographers? Still, it's sometimes the most intriguing line to be found in the book.

A variant claim or confession, aptly invoking the law in a crime novel, occurs on the copyright page of *Original Sin*: 'P. D. James is hereby indentified [*sic*] as author of this work in accordance with section 77 of the Copyright, Designs and Patents Act 1988.'

For all those dazzling girls who lit up the drab offices, some of them debs, obviously not there for the money, but happy to do a prenuptial stint in a socially acceptable environment, it's someone else I best remember. Mrs Holden, small, neat and middle-aged, who made the morning coffee and brought it round to us. True, she was with us for years, whereas secretaries came and (for the most part swiftly) went. Mrs Holden was a true lady. She didn't consider it lowering to serve out coffee (she knew it was the high point of the day); since it was she who did it, nor could we.

One day I happened to be in the room of our chairman (*sic*), Mrs Norah Smallwood, when Mrs Holden arrived with the coffee. We were about to publish a first book of memoirs by Dirk Bogarde, a discovery of Mrs Smallwood's, and it was known that another famous actor, Kenneth More, had a book of memoirs due out at the same time. 'Now, Mrs Holden,' said Mrs Smallwood briskly, 'If you were in a bookshop and you saw books by Dirk Bogarde and Kenneth More, which one would you buy?' After a moment's pause—would she buy either?—'Kenneth More,' replied Mrs Holden. (She was clearly too busy to listen to office chit-chat.) 'Oh,' said Mrs Smallwood, 'I do hope you haven't chipped my cup, Mrs Holden.'

General Sir John Hackett has died. We published his first book, *I Was a Stranger*, which tells of how, when he was stranded in Arnhem after the unsuccessful airborne landing of 1944, the local people gave him shelter. Since he couldn't speak the language, and any German interrogator would expect him to, they pinned a badge on him, bearing the Dutch words signifying deafness. Someone designed a picture of the badge for the back cover of his book. Soon after it appeared we had a letter from Holland which expressed the sender's warm appreciation of the book, and politely pointed out that the inscription on the badge as represented on the jacket was incorrect: instead of 'hard of hearing' the words there meant 'hard of whoring'. I don't think anyone mentioned this to Sir John.

Second thoughts . . . The MIT Press wish us to know that the title of a book listed in their 1994 catalogue, *Big Dummy's Guide to the Internet*, has been changed to *Everybody's Guide to the Internet*. So that's what they think of everybody?

※

THE 'Personals' at the back of *The New York Review of Books* are what one would expect of the paper's intellectual status. '*Stand Corrected* is the only spanking magazine edited by a Vassar woman.' This continues, 'also exquisitely designed (includes thrilling catalog of spanking erotica)'. Price $21.95; brochure only $5. In an adjoining column we are offered 'DELUXE MASSAGE-ROLEPLAY by beautiful natural blonde Austrian lady. Central Park South.'

Austrian ladies are famous for their brains, and this one, like many Austrian ladies, is beautiful as well. The winning combination features in a later issue: 'ALL FETISHES DOMINATION/SUBMISSION FANTASIES explored by Ivy League educated Goddess.'

The nearest the *Times Literary Supplement*'s classifieds have come to this is: 'London, the Penn Club. Friendly b. & b. with long established Quaker connections. Situated historic Bloomsbury, very close to British Museum. Direct links with Heathrow. A secure, quiet base, ideal for persons travelling alone.'

THE highest kind of teacher, Kierkegaard says in an intricate passage on religious philosophy, is the one who gives the pupil not only the truth but also the condition for understanding it. 'All instruction depends upon the presence, in the last analysis, of the requisite condition; if this is lacking, no teacher can do anything.' For then the teacher would have to re-create the pupil at the outset, and this, if it is to be done, can be done only by God himself.

In our more mundane educational system, or so you might think, the condition for understanding would be created along with the understanding. (I avoid Kierkegaard's word 'truth', because not everybody believes there is such a thing; understanding, unlike truth, can be assumed to be, very often, incomplete: that is why it is capable of growth.) A literary work, if it is worth studying, surely offers that condition, the possibility of it, conveys it to the teacher as 'part of the parcel' which he, if he is worth listening to, 'undoes' and passes on spontaneously. What you teach and how you teach are as inseparable as style and substance. This process—for which one can hardly find any other name than 'teaching'—doesn't seem to feature in Diploma or B.Ed. courses, but is of the essence. It may even save teachers from violence (or at least adverse assessments) at the hands of disaffected pupils.

'He who can, does. He who cannot, teaches.' This may be true of the lower reaches of the profession, but is otherwise a big untruth. More accurate would be: He who can, teaches. He who cannot, writes books.

In all the present debate on education, nothing is said about teachers needing a special talent, in its origins perhaps innate rather than acquired: a talent for persuasive communication. I suppose it wouldn't do.

In Singapore I tried to get a young lecturer's contract renewed on the grounds that though he hadn't published—the great stumbling block—he was a first-rate teacher, enthusiastic and much admired by the students. But the Vice-Chancellor, a shade ruefully, wanted something more objective: 'We are all good teachers, aren't we?'

This wasn't altogether the case. At about the same time there was a lecturer in political science, imported from Taiwan (technically an expatriate therefore, but he didn't *look* like one), whose command of English was extremely poor. He had a doctorate from an American university, but his thesis, it turned out, had been written in Latin. He was accused of sexual harassment during a tutorial, and after a brief investigation—the only witness was the girl's boyfriend—he resigned. Quite possibly the girl had misunderstood his linguistic intentions.

Teacher training? I can think of one useful thing: a short course in elocution, how to speak clearly and with as much volume as the circumstances require.

'WHY NOT BE A WRITER? As a freelance writer, you can earn very good money in your spare time, writing the stories, articles, books, scripts etc. that editors and publishers want. Millions of pounds are paid annually in fees and royalties. Earning your share can be fun, profitable and creatively most fulfilling . . .'
    One client writes: 'Since enrolling I have had over 100 items published and earned £8960. The best thing is that I still find it all great fun.' (I bet you do.)
    Another client: 'It used to be hard work selling my articles. Now editors call me and ask if I will write for them.'
    And—but that's enough. Let's sign up with The Writers Bureau (Freepost, Manchester) right away. They even guarantee to refund the course fees in full if you haven't earned them from published writings by the time you finish the course. So why not be a writer? You can't lose. (Who the devil is this happy 'you'?)

A novelist living in the West Midlands advertises his wares: 'Engaging heroines. Plausible heroes. Virgins converted. Villains thwarted. Erotica espoused. Hearts rent asunder. Desire and greed embraced. Obsessive lust a speciality.' Address, telephone and fax numbers given.

With such a gift for words—'virgins converted', 'erotica espoused'—he's going to do really well. And find it all great fun.

This checks with a recent Peanuts strip. Snoopy the dog is busy on one of his novels: 'Everything was calm and peaceful. Suddenly, it all happened.' Lucy sticks her oar in: 'What do you mean, it all happened? This isn't exciting enough. You have to make it more exciting.' So Snoopy rewrites: 'Suddenly, it all happened again.'

February 1996. Reporting the rumpus between Random House (well-known publishing company) and Joan Collins (well-known actress), a writer in *The Times* comments: 'Book commissioning and editing, once seen as cardigan-and-cocoa occupations, have been unveiled as complex, brutal, zappy affairs. Thanks to Joan Collins we have seen the big-cigar decisions modern publishers take, the highly complex discussions which must take place before a word of a novel is written.'

In brief, Random House wants the return of a $1.2 million advance already paid to Miss Collins on the grounds that her new novel isn't up to scratch, while Miss Collins wants the remaining $2.8 million of the advance paid to her on the grounds that she has delivered the said novel to them complete.

The loss of several million dollars won't bring Random House crashing down. (That's to say, I trust the company will go on paying me my paltry pension.) We know that publishing is big business these days, and big business is 'brutal'. If publishers deal in garbage they must expect to get their hands dirty. But what was that snide remark about 'cardigan-and-cocoa'? At least in my time, the Dark Ages I suppose, we assumed that our authors were able to write, more or less, and we knew how to draw up contracts. As for those 'highly complex discussions', just think of the complex discussions that take place in the poet's mind before he finishes a line, or in the prose-writer's before he completes a sentence.

But best to sit back and enjoy yet another real-life soap opera. If you allow your feelings to show, these fellows will say you're a superannuated old git, envious of the exciting times in which they live and move and have their lawsuits and severance pay.

Later. It appears that Miss Collins will end up with $3 million. She has thanked the jurors and said how thrilled she is with the outcome, which has reinforced her belief in justice. (When we get what we want, suddenly there's justice in the world.) Outside publishing, the general rejoicing bears some resemblance to the dancing in the streets when the verdict against Oscar Wilde was announced. 'Now Barabbas was a publisher', and not a very competent one at that.

A publisher advertises for someone to fill a 'key role' in the firm. An interest in books 'would be an advantage, but not essential'. On the other hand, 'you must have a thorough knowledge of WordPerfect 5.1, and speeds of 100/80'. True, a key role.

It is said that when Simon & Schuster were publishing a children's book called *Mr Dan the Bandage Man*, they conceived the stunt of enclosing a packet of Band-Aids in each copy of the book. They wired the manufacturers, Johnson & Johnson: 'Send one million Band-Aids immediately.' Johnson & Johnson wired back: 'Band-Aids on the way. What the hell happened to you?'

A NEW novel, according to a critic, 'can be dull reading'; at the same time the author has a 'genius for the ordinary'. The Reviewer gives, and the Reviewer takes away, blessed be the name of the Reviewer.

'After fifty pages I found my hand stealing towards this book at every spare moment.' No, it wasn't a naughty book, not in the least. (It was Kingsley Amis's last novel.) But are reviewers in the habit of devoting only their spare moments to the job?

A curious review of a novel set in Belfast, so harrowing 'that it turns your knuckles white'. The villain is given to knee-capping, which may explain the reviewer's comment that another character, a female, is 'in love in a weak-at-the-knees sort of way'.

The characterization, 'a wrist-strengthening novel', is to be taken as a commendation, implying that it keeps you turning the pages (some 700 of them in this case). More explicit was Ambrose Bierce's comment on something he had been reading: 'The covers of this book are too far apart.'

But pity reviewers! Such desperate measures are they driven to, such frantic gymnastics. 'A lot of flagellation and a matching literary-exquisite style.' 'A funny, sad, nasty little gem of a novel.' Even more enticing: 'It's canny and camp, tender but butch, trashy, sexy, witty and informative. In other words, it's not just important, it's silly.' The novel: 'the one bright book of life'?

'All affection for chimpanzees and for humanity is lost after reading this book, but that is a small price to pay for the vigorous and imaginative entertainment it provides.' I'm all for entertainment, but perhaps not at that ('small') price. Strikes me as the sort of thing Johnson had in mind in a review of his: 'Many of the books which now crowd the world may be justly suspected to be written for the sake of some invisible order of beings, for surely they are of no use to any of the corporeal inhabitants of the world.'

Herewith my current nominee for The Most Incredible Book Review of the Year.

The subject, a novel, concerns a serial killer of young homosexual men, who keeps his victims as companions, 'stroking and talking to and raping their rotting bodies until they disintegrate, and then cutting them to pieces'. The reviewer made herself a sandwich in the middle of her reading, 'and it was a mistake'. The novel, she confides, was the first to make her feel physically sick. Yet it held her attention 'utterly rapt until its ghastly end'. (Takes some doing, remaining rapt while vomiting.) Lots of people would hate the book, thinking it 'unpleasant, offensive, vile'. Is it? 'Well yes, of course it is.' (The phrase 'of course' often means 'so what?') For the writing is 'beautiful', the author is witty and intelligent, and her exploration of what might drive a man to do things 'gruesome beyond belief' is 'disturbing' and 'intriguing' and 'may or may not be close to some sort of truth'. (Some sort of beauty may be some sort of truth: that's all you need to know.) The reviewer then wonders whether she would have felt the same had the author been a man, for in that case she 'might have found the book alarming for a whole host of other reasons'. (Reasons not given.) Perhaps she was 'seeking comfort in the fact that this tale of lurid homosexual destructive fantasy was indeed merely fantasy'—because a woman had written it. (This line of thought, apparently adumbrating a new law of literature, or maybe of life, leaves me baffled.) And she concludes by returning in memory to her sandwich: the book in question, however shocking, is 'a book to devour. But not while you are eating.'

In its way this review is useful, as one would expect of the paper of record in which it appeared. It warns us not to devour when our mouths are full. It warns us that the conscientious reviewer's lot is not always a happy one.

'Everything, in the world, exists to end up in a book': Mallarmé. That would account for the vast number of books in existence. But is so much in the world really that sick?

Beat the drum! In India those who concern themselves with garbage belong to a low caste known as pariahs. A horrid term, you might think. Yet something of a euphemism, in that the word 'pariah' comes from the Tamil for 'drummer', an allusion to a more genteel activity of the caste—beating the drum at certain festivals.

Derwent May says that while he was literary editor of *The Listener* he once failed to persuade Hugh Trevor-Roper to review a batch of history books because at the time this gentleman found himself unable to read anything except the most beautiful prose. (We can assume that his idea of the beautiful differed from that invoked above.) An excellent reason for declining a commission. Naturally it helps if you have other sources of income.

True. And if you carry on like this, you will confine yourself to reviewing only books which you think truly valuable and those of which it can at least be claimed that they are unexceptionable. Bear in mind what Julian Barnes said in an interview with Christopher Hawtree: 'Freelance! That grand word which all too often means that there are two people who might give you some reviewing.'

❧

'IF we abuse children we abuse our own future.' This factor is seen as a potent condemnation, a sound, unsentimental argument having vaguely but tellingly to do with market forces, productivity, consumer goods. And carrying an air of practical folksy wisdom, as though to say, If you cut your nose off you will spite your face. It might be thought sufficient to say, If we abuse children, we abuse children.

Accounts of educational reforms proposed by the political parties customarily come to the same grand climax: 'and in this way we shall strengthen the country's economic future'. The bottom line is the top line.

'It is now undeniable that the arts are not only good for trade but they are trade': Melvyn Bragg in *The Times*. Undeniably, but do we always have to defend things on the same incongruous grounds?

On camera, an earnest young person, emitting decency from every pore, declares that if Shell cleans up its act, ceases to consort with disreputable regimes and shows a proper care for the environment, we shall all begin to love it, and it will make even greater profits. 'Enlightened self-interest!' she exclaims joyously.

Enlightened self-interest. It sounds delightful. Just what the world needs. Except that having it both ways rarely lasts. Enlightenment is the junior partner in these alliances and, if interest decrees, before long a sleeping partner.

We say that things are proved on the pulse. Then we tell people they shouldn't judge by their own experience. For this is 'anecdotal', not representative, and doesn't count in the scheme of things.

A rail company dismisses complaints of overcrowding on their trains by recourse to metaphysics: 'more a matter of perception than of reality'. Their customers are not representative, they merely *perceive* that they are uncomfortable.

It has taken a scientific study to establish that a stag experiences severe stress (if not distress) when hunted. Science is wonderful. A supporter of stag-hunting counters with the claim that a scientific study in progress will establish that a hunted stag does not experience stress (let alone distress).

Some while back a study was made of attitudes among Thai peasants. They were required to respond to 'a series of standardized stimuli', i.e. to complete simple sentences. One of the sentences began: 'When something worries you, you . . .' A majority of those interviewed supplied words signifying 'feel worried'.

Nothing, it seems, is less obvious than the obvious. Can this state of affairs have something to do with a proposition advanced by Malcolm Bowie when contrasting literary theory with literary text? 'The concept of difficulty can conduce towards a life of ease.'

❧

HAMAS clerics promise the young men recruited as suicide bombers a special paradise where each will be presented with seventy-two virgin brides. Clearly a richer life than they can expect on earth. No wonder there are thousands of volunteers.

Bachelors are preferred, we hear, since a married man might give the game away by bidding his wife too feeling a farewell. ('I may be some time.') And his wife might not be too pleased about those seventy-two rivals.

Recently a twelve-year-old Israeli girl has been quoted as finding the arrangement—eternal life in paradise—a bit unfair.

Swallowing a camel and choking on a gnat; or, Observe the niceties, never mind the nastinesses. A report from Iran has it that young women condemned to death are raped beforehand because religious authorities decree that virgins can enter paradise in spite of having been lawfully executed. (Virginity can be tantamount to cheating.) So the women go through a form of temporary marriage to an appointed male—chosen by lottery from among members of the firing squad and attendant officials—and, whether to palliate pain or preclude pleasure is not made plain, are injected with a tranquillizer before consummation. Moreover, on the following day a man of religion writes out a marriage certificate and sends it to the grieving family, together with a box of sweets.

The custom of defloration prior to execution, usually the gaoler's perk, goes back a long way in our history. But the marriage certificate and the box of sweets are distinctively modern features.

It seems widows in Afghanistan have a hard time too. They can't remarry, they are not allowed to work, being females—and they are blamed for their husbands' deaths because they failed to pray hard enough for them.

More amusing—it happened a long time ago—is the story of the Caliph who ordered the destruction of the library of Alexandria on thoroughly logical grounds. Either the books said the same thing as the Koran, in which case they were superfluous, or else they said something different, in which case they were wrong and pernicious.

Also, on the face of it, amusing is that paper bags are outlawed in present-day Afghanistan because discarded pages of the Koran might be recycled and turned into bags. Yet one can see the point there, a nicety worth observing.

The narrator of Salman Rushdie's *The Moor's Last Sigh* remarks that somehow or other his parents had been cured of religion. 'Where's their medicine, their priest-poison-beating anti-venene? Bottle it, for pity's sake, and send it round the world!' Straight from the author's heart.

The French philosopher Alain said that when he was asked by some pious person what he thought of religion, he replied, 'Religion is a fairy tale which, like all fairy tales, is full of meaning. And no one asks if fairy tales are true.'

Religion has effects, and effects are often attended by side-effects. When we were still on speaking terms, the doctor told me that the painkillers he had prescribed might cause constipation but the anti-inflammatory drug he also prescribed was likely to cause diarrhoea, and so the two would cancel out. In fact they didn't; as if by a gentlemen's agreement, they took it in turns. It seems that the side-effects are sometimes more effective than the effects.

Rushdie might prefer another comment of Alain's: 'Apart from errors of taste, which give themselves away, the history of art equals a succession of enveloped truths; and it is primarily because of this that humanity amounts to something.'

There's a sticky proviso there. But it isn't exactly errors of taste that Rushdie has been held guilty of. Bad taste is hardly a concept in religion. All the same, one wouldn't be too surprised to hear the resurrection of Christ termed an unfortunate error of judgement or the virgin birth an instance of downright bad taste.

'Chain a dog if you want him to become savage. A man who is bound to a fixed creed naturally becomes a persecutor': Mark Rutherford.

Hitherto the naughtiness of Buddhist monks in Thailand, largely confined to occasional bottom-pinching on the buses, has gone unreported. Of late they have been in the news, and naturally not by virtue of their virtuousness. 'Seduced by the new consumer culture,' says the press—an odd way of accounting for rape, murder and necrophilia—while witnesses less detached from the scene murmur testily against the short skirts and see-through blouses of foreign ladies.

A notice outside a temple in Bangkok: 'It is forbidden to enter a woman even a foreigner if dressed as a man.'

The snake in the Garden: 'the little lecturer,' Heine called it, the 'bluestocking without legs'.

'Ye shall be as gods'—
Thank you, but it hardly seems
A tempting prospect.

❧

ANTHOLOGISTS are getting a rough deal, notably from single-issue critics. One, himself a specialist in 'true stories' of the paranormal, contends that an anthology of the supernatural ought to confine itself to accounts of the unaccountable. Another, the director of a conservation organization, complains that an anthology on the subject of creatures doesn't give sufficient prominence to impassioned defenders of endangered species and animal-rights campaigners. A gay reviewer grumbles because an anthology of friendship is deficient in homoerotic material.

A matter for gratitude: that when the subject was death, literary editors couldn't find deceased reviewers to put the anthologist right.

Three years after the publication of *The Oxford Book of the Supernatural*, a letter arrives from Johannesburg: 'I am writing on behalf of my mother, who is constantly being attacked by ghosts every other night. The ghosts press on her chest so she cannot breathe, touch her feet etc. This has been happening for approx a year and a half now and no local "fundis" seem to be able to help. Do you have any ideas or information that would help her, as these attacks are very upsetting and disturbing. We are desperate for your help and would gratefully appreciate any assistance. PS These ghosts follow you to different locations.'

It sounds like a classic case of incumbency or possession by an incubus, but it wouldn't do to say so. The reference to 'fundis' is cryptic; the dictionary defines 'fundi', from Swahili, as a person skilled in repairing or maintaining machinery. Do mechanics double as exorcists? At all events the poor woman needs the physician or the divine more than the anthologist. The thought doesn't prevent me feeling inadequate, even guilty. And—that PS—a shade apprehensive.

※

THE 'people' in Kafka's last story, 'Josephine the Singer; or The Mouse People', live in a hostile world, are constantly on the go, meet trouble with a certain practical cunning and a consoling smile. They are tenacious and hopeful, used to suffering; they can behave childishly, extravagantly, yet in a sense they are prematurely old. They are totally unmusical, though music has been known to them since antiquity and is mentioned in legend.

Josephine is their singer, albeit what she does might better be described as squeaking ('pfeifen': J. P. Stern insists on 'whistling', which preserves the human connection): this is a special skill of theirs, or rather a typical 'sign of life'. It may be that Josephine isn't really much of a singer, but they wouldn't *want* a real singer. By her singing (squeaking, piping, whistling) she believes she gives them strength in times of danger, and so she unaccountably does, though her singing, it has to be said, is itself a source of danger: it attracts the enemy, and many of those assembled to listen have been killed.

Much of what is said of these people can be applied to literal mice, a species both vulnerable and hardy, generation treading on the heels of generation, but we can't believe that the story is a rodent equivalent of *Watership Down*. So perhaps this is a fable concerning the relationship between the individual and the community: Josephine thinks she protects the community, the community thinks it protects Josephine; by no means work-shy, she asks to be relieved of all duties outside singing in recognition of her unique status, a request the community turns down. Or: Josephine the singer 'equals' Kafka the writer, a man who put all his living energy into writing while 'wasting away' in other areas. ('I am made of literature, I am nothing else.') And when the writer falls silent, as does the singer in the story, the nation, the public, will very soon get over the loss. It is said that Kafka, correcting the proofs of the story on his deathbed, cried a little.

To me the story of the mouse people sounds much like a story about the Jews of the diaspora: above all, though not exclusively, for this is the universalizing author of *The Trial* and 'The Metamorphosis'. Allowing that many things make such an interpretation plausible—and that 'Jews, too, when you come to think of it, are human beings, metonyms of the human race'—Stern claims that one notable attribute militates against it: the 'mouse nation' has no interest in history, whereas the Jews have never forgotten what happened (the destruction of the Temple) 1900-odd years after the event. The narrator, it's true, states that 'generally speaking, the study of history is something we neglect completely'. But in 1924 Jews in Europe might be thought to possess little in the way of national history as distinct from their momentous religious past, or feel disinclined to dwell on international history and how it had treated them. The text is curiously ambiguous on the point. Josephine, having disappeared from sight, is deemed 'a minor episode in the unending history of our people'; and she will happily vanish into 'the countless throng of the heroes of our people'. (Heroes are the stuff of history.) The following (and closing) words, however, seem to reverse direction: '. . . and soon, since we do not go in for history, enjoy the even greater release of being forgotten like all her brethren'. Rather than either/or, it may be both.

Imported notions or considerations may distort a reader's interpretation, but we cannot always dump them at the border. In this instance a number of interpretations are possible or plausible or even persuasive, and co-exist, no matter how incompatible one with another they appear when mooted severally. The tale is 'representative' with a vengeance! Stern considers it Kafka's most serene, only serene, story. To me it is disquieting, foreboding. Soon after finishing it, as though he had called down a curse on himself, Kafka was—

if not squeaking or whistling—whispering and rasping. Treatment for tuberculosis of the larynx would cost an awful lot: 'Josephine will have to help out a little.' Three months later he was dead.

Not easy to imagine Kafka a star among Emerson's 'Representative Men', heroic though he was in his way.

And yet, Kafka as representative son: 'All parents want to do is drag one down to them, back to the old days from which one longs to free oneself and escape; they do it out of love, of course, and that's what makes it so horrible.' (21 November 1912.)

As representative office-worker: 'In one of the corridors along which I always walk to reach my typist, there used to be a coffin-like trolley for the moving of files and documents, and each time I passed it I felt as though it had been made for me, and was waiting for me . . . My desk at the office was certainly never tidy, but now it is littered with a chaotic pile of papers and files; I may just know the things that lie on top, but lower down I suspect nothing but horrors. Sometimes I look around the office with an expression that no one would ever have believed possible in an office.' (1 November and 3 December 1912.)

As representative lodger: 'The walls are really terribly thin; to my landlady's sorrow I stopped the striking-clock in my room . . . but then the striking-clock next door strikes all the louder . . . but I cannot play the tyrant and demand that this clock be stopped as well. It would be no good anyway, there is always bound to be a certain amount of whispering, the doorbell is bound to ring; the other lodger coughed twice yesterday, by today it was more often, his cough hurts me more than it does him.' (11 February 1915.)

As representative lover: 'I was unhappy about your illness, but now my true nature is revealed: I would have been unhappier still had you been well, and not written to me.' (17 November 1912.)

As representative writer: 'I have no literary interests, but am made of literature, I am nothing else, and cannot be anything else . . . Not a bent for writing, not a bent, but my entire self. A bent can be uprooted and crushed. But this is what I am.' (14 and 24 August 1913. From *Letters to Felice*, translated by James Stern and Elisabeth Duckworth.)

That mysterious aphorism of Kafka's, his most difficult saying. To the effect that original sin, the ancient wrong committed by man, consists in the complaint that man makes and never ceases making: that a wrong has been done to man, that it was upon man that original sin was committed. That is—I think—the sin is our complaining about the sin. 'There's no justice in the world.'

※

INTRODUCING E. M. Cioran's *A Short History of Decay* (*Précis de Décomposition*, 1949; translated by Richard Howard), Michael Tanner states, 'All good aphoristic writing is tiring to read, because one has to do most of the writer's work for him; he supplies a sentence, the serious reader turns it into a paragraph.' *Really* tiring? More tiring than struggling through a paragraph, a page, and turning it into a sentence?

Think of the effort demanded by those writers who believe, or have been induced to suppose, that length is the sign of depth. The notion afflicts even detective novels. An ingenious plot, sufficiently differentiated characters, attractive or the reverse, some action and some suspense: that ought to be enough. But no, there have to be wodges of psychologizing, sociologizing, history, topography, lifted from the fashionable 'disciplines' of the day. The attempt to make crime stories into literature almost invariably ruins them as entertainment, their *raison d'être*. Much the same has happened to science fiction, propelled into social comment, feminist agitprop, Gaian doom, cyberpunk, technological dystopia (chips with everything), violence, squalor and disgust. Thus losing the point of the genre: imagination and adventure.

In fact Cioran writes at excessive length, and is tiring to read because he does too much of the readers' work for them, and in so doing blunts the point of his pen. We resent what we feel as bludgeoning, we reckon we deserve the rapier.

Nevertheless, herewith a few of Cioran's aphorisms, timely ripped from the context which commonly elaborates and spoils. Or, a few paragraphs turned into sentences.

'A man who loves a god unduly forces other men to love his god, eager to exterminate them if they refuse.' (Loving unduly? Not all decent people can rise to a Cordelia-like exactitude: I love your godhead according to my bond; no more nor less.) More generally, 'Once a man loses his *faculty of indifference* he becomes a potential murderer.' No 'wavering mind', no Hamlet, 'was ever pernicious'; suppress certitudes—Cioran is certain of this—'and you recover paradise'. Possibly so, but we would like to hear more of this recoverable paradise. 'I dream of an Eleusis of disabused hearts, of a lucid Mystery, without gods and without the vehemences of illusions': a procession of oxymorons, hopes raised and shattered in the same breath, truly a dream. (We have a right to dreams.)

Later this thought manifests itself in a preference for prostitutes over philosophers. The prostitute is detached, open to everything, 'espousing her client's mood and ideas', protean, ready to be sad or gay (i.e. essentially indifferent). Thou best philosopher—a model of behaviour. If this seems bizarre, then remember that frivolity—'the pursuit of the superficial by those who have discerned the impossibility of any certitude, and have conceived a disgust for such things'—is 'a privilege and an art', and no one attains to it straight off.

'Compared to music, mysticism, and poetry, philosophical activity proceeds from a diminished impulse and a suspect depth, prestigious only for the timid and tepid.' (NB: 'To make fun of philosophy is truly to philosophize': Pascal.) There isn't enough of humanity's suffering in philosophy; and 'almost all the philosophers came to a *good end*: that is the supreme argument against philosophy'. All its thoughts, put together, fail to make a single page equivalent to 'one of Job's exclamations, of Macbeth's terrors, or the altitude of one of Bach's cantatas'. For the philosopher is 'the enemy of disaster', sane, prudent, and null. We prefer the company 'of an old plague victim, of a poet learned in every lunacy, and of a musician whose sublimity transcends the sphere of the heart'. There's no disputing that good taste.

'The effect a book has on us is real only if we crave to imitate its plot, to kill if its hero kills, to be jealous if he is jealous, to take sick and die if he suffers and expires.' This, the opposite of the cathartic theory (the tragic hero dies, we feel all the better for it), lays a fearful burden on the serious reader, but is a change from the common idea that reading has no effect whatsoever.

To die . . . In his first book, with the oxymoronic title *On the Heights of Despair*, Cioran noted how strange it was to think that, just turning twenty-one, he was already a specialist in the question of death. There, life was 'the privilege of mediocre people'. Here, 'Life belongs to dolts; and it is in order to fill out the life they have not had that we have invented *the lives of the poets*.' (See, for instance, the biographies of Thomas Mann.)

The abjection of ownership, including clothes, gets 'between us and nothingness'. It is because we go round dressed that we entertain the notion of immortality: 'How can we die when we wear a tie?' (People have been known to die with their boots on. But hyperbole is an accepted form of grim humour.)

The idea of progress makes asses of us all. We used to tremble in caves, now we tremble in skyscrapers. 'Our capital of misery remains intact down the ages, yet we have one advantage over our ancestors: that of having *invested* our capital better, since our disaster is better organized.' That's marvellously well said. And any metaphor drawn from stocks and shares is bound to command wide respect.

Such is Cioran's rhetoric—hot and cold, brutal and fastidious, a 'calm torrent' in Michael Tanner's oxymoron—that you cannot always tell whether he is extolling or execrating; if you decide for the latter you won't often be wrong. Compared with him, Nietzsche (though, like Socrates, he didn't come to a conspicuously good end) is a sober carefree youth. Cioran's Superman, for all his roistering, couldn't endure to live once, let alone repeat the cycle. 'All our humiliations come from the fact that we cannot bring ourselves to die of hunger.' And—hardly such good company as that adduced above —'I have more esteem for a concierge who hangs himself than for a living poet': Ecclesiastes' living dog and dead lion turned upside down.

To my surprise—clearly I am no serious reader—I realize that I reviewed the translation when it first came out, in 1975, remarking, apropos of Cioran's reputed lucidity, that 'Alas, in him *lucide* aspires towards the condition of *suicide*.'

Still, it may not often have been thought but rarely has it been so well expressed. All of Cioran, put together, is less lowering than a few pages of a smart, standard, shabby novel produced by some calculating friend of disaster.

※

THE *fait divers*, Jean Baudrillard has said, offers the chance of 'being there without being there'. And in the seventeenth century the grammarian Gilles Ménage envisaged a book, 'fort curieux', made up of the 'things which have been said only once'.

Mr James Pettit Andrews, an eighteenth-century amateur of *faits divers* and anecdotes, including things which shouldn't have been said even once, warns translators to be cautious about their title-pages. He cites a Mr Thomas Cockman, who rendered Cicero's *De Officiis* ('Concerning Duties') as *Concerning Offices*—as if the work were in the line of Mr Jeremy Lewis's more recent *Chatto Book of Office Life*.

In fact the errors of translation listed are few and minor in the extreme when set against the possibilities offered by our modern internationalism. The most striking is ascribed to a French student, at work on the passage, 'Erat homo qui habebat manum aridam' (Matthew 12: 'There was a man which had his hand withered'). This he translated as 'Il y eut un homme qui avoit une méchante haridelle': 'there was a man who had a worn-out nag'. Recourse to a Latin dictionary—in the time of our anecdotist everyone knew Latin, of course—informs me of a word 'mannus', signifying a coach-horse. The miracle suffers little from the misunderstanding. 'Stretch forth thine nag . . . and it was restored whole.'

The M. Ménage mentioned above once found his carriage held up by that of a gentleman who owed him a thousand crowns (mille écus). The debtor cried out, 'Mille excuses, Monsieur, mille excuses!', to which M. Ménage rejoined coldly, 'Mille écus, Monsieur, mille écus!'

Mr Andrews has a delicate mind, and—by rendering them incomprehensible—spoils many of the more promising stories he proposes to convey. An exception, possibly inspired by respect for class distinctions, concerns a letter written to Queen Caroline (of England) by the Duchess of Orleans, in which the latter tells how she got the better of an impostor, a protégée of Mme de Maintenon, by advising her that her mother was 'une putain' and, if she ever again called herself Countess Palatine, 'Je te ferai couper les jupes au ras du cul'. A footnote explains: 'The words are coarse, but a *princess* writes them to a *Queen*, and they are *not* translated.'

Incidentally, the spurious countess was so frightened by the thought of having her skirts cut short at her *cul* that she took ill and died a few days afterwards.

A 'worn-out nag' and the Foreign Poet. While much translated poetry of recent decades has been excellent, and we should be poorer without it, there is a substratum in which a good deal must have got lost, even though the 'story' (often a sad one) survives. The result can be characterless, contextless, obscurely momentous, inconsequent, bathetic, and inadvertently comic. Two examples follow, by no means among the worst, possibly a shade endearing.

Trees (1)

From time to time I gaze at the trees outside.
Yesterday I gazed at the trees outside,
Tomorrow I expect to gaze at the trees.
This I did last year, this I shall do next year.
No doubt the trees are beautiful to view,
I muse as I doff my conical cap.
Also, it strikes me as I stroke my beard,
The trees can grow rather tedious.

*

At this point, incautiously absorbed in the
Joy of words, the poet was assailed by a band
Of seeming brigands emerging from the trees.
Their intent was purely to rid the world
Of vapid and unproductive lives, of drones
Who neither sowed nor reaped. These included
Scholars wearing long beards and high hats.

The story shows how one should never relax.
Even the trees outside will need to be heeded.

Trees (2)

I peer at the trees outside
This is my present labour
I am looking for a parrot
Lost by a grieving neighbour.

Alas the parrot is green
(Which is all I know of the parrot)
And all the trees too are green
(Indeed they are all too green).

Though I long to be its saviour
However hard I have tried
The parrot is not to be seen
As I peer at the trees outside.

It's a bright windy morning, and the poplars outside are dancing. Or it might be brawling. Behind and to one side, the weeping willow, its skirts decently trailing the ground, is quite still, except for an occasional tremor, as if discreetly wiping a tear away.

Ruskin, who invented the term, obviously wasn't keen on the 'pathetic fallacy': a 'falseness', he claimed, in our impression of external things. (And it must be said for the poems quoted above that they exhibit little sign of this particular solecism.) But if nature, who for better or worse shares her life with us, doesn't lend herself to metaphor, doesn't oblige with such fellow feelings, what is she there for? 'O Lady! we receive but what we give,/And in our life alone does Nature live': Coleridge.

※

A MOONCALF introducing a crackbrain's book on a madman . . . It's only from the madman that we get any sort of lucid, compelling (almost compelling) sense: *On Nietzsche*, by Georges Bataille, introduced by Sylvère Lotringer.

It is not Heidegger's writings that have cast a shadow over his reputation, we hear; it is his Nazi connections and his silence on the Holocaust. It is not Derrida's writings that have cast a shadow over his reputation; it is his discipleship or connection with Heidegger. So we gather from someone who gives the impression of knowing and understanding the two intellectuals and their work rather well, and who is able to declare: 'Derrida's body of work has transformed the dominant methods of thinking in all the humanities and social sciences. Academically, this has led to nothing less than a reorganization of the teaching in university departments in Britain and America.'

It is true that Heidegger's Nazi connections and Derrida's discipleship are readily grasped, far more readily than their writings, and thus serve to 'marginalize' them, if not get rid of them. Personally I have no great objection to that end, only to those means. But let's not be ungrateful. Now perhaps the university departments can re-reorganize themselves.

Didier Eribon begins his biography of Michel Foucault by pointing to the seemingly paradoxical nature of the undertaking, in that Foucault had challenged the notion of 'the author', 'thereby dismissing the very possibility of a biographical study'. Even so, Foucault is, 'in short', an author, despite himself. (The little phrase 'in short' must encapsulate a very long and tricky argument.) There was another problem: some people worried that homosexuality would come up, and might be misunderstood. But Eribon was resolved to 'resist the subtle forms of repression and censorship that await all writers'—the writer, above all the biographer, as hero!—and were to be resisted all the more firmly in the case of Foucault. One appreciates the difficulties; or, more truly, this frank admission of them.

At the end of the book Eribon tells of a man who challenged the 'rumour' that Foucault had died of AIDS by printing a brief item in a newspaper: 'We are still astonished by the virulence of this rumour. As if it were necessary for Foucault to have died in shame.' This man was an admirer, and imagined he was doing the right thing, defending Foucault against a campaign intended to discredit him as a thinker. But, Eribon continues, 'it was an ill-considered text', peculiarly so in a newspaper called *Libération*. A deluge of protests descended on the writer's head: what was shameful in dying of AIDS? and so forth. Eribon shows a degree of what we must deem *brave* compassion: 'I know that every day of his life he regrets the blunder, and I do not want to be among his attackers.'

A sad, admonitory story—the poor fellow regrets his blunder every day of his life!—and a rather alarming one. Foucault has been praised as a heretic; but of course there are heresies and heresies. Censorship is an evil, except when it's wholly justified. (Wouldn't the newspaper called *Libération* have been justified in censoring that brief, misguided item?) The underground burgeons into the overground, a handful of rebels swells into a large flock of sheep.

I was reminded of a miscalculation in a book of mine, in which I rashly broached the question of a possible link between television violence and real-life crime, suggesting that important public figures in the entertainment world had taken a too casual, scornfully dismissive view of the possibility. How could they be so *sure*? In a later passage on the Moors murders, I quoted a police inspector as saying, apropos of paedophile pornography, 'Today's looker is tomorrow's doer.' One reviewer, already narked by the *lèse-majesté* exhibited towards those important public figures, seized on this with glee. I had produced a 'star witness' of my own: 'For Enright, apparently, such police testimony constitutes conclusive proof.' Never mind that I offered the inspector's remark, not as conclusive proof (I was at some pains to grant that such proof might never be forthcoming), but as a succinctly expressed proposition, one not to be rejected out of hand.

In its smaller way, my blunder was comparable to the 'ill-considered text' of Foucault's well-wisher. Incidentally, the reviewer was a university lecturer in English, and the review appeared—not in a paper called *Libération* or the like—in *The Times Educational Supplement*.

※

MANY a man, overwearied by it, may shun it with dread—Coleridge observes in his notebooks—but woe to him for whom the question of evil is without interest. They deserve to be scourged with lofty scorn, 'those Critics who laugh at the discussion of old Questions—God, Right & Wrong, Necessity & Arbitrement, Evil, &c.' The massed ranks of social workers rise up in indignation.

They get their revenge a few months later, when Coleridge confides: 'What a beautiful Thing Urine is, in a Pot, brown yellow, transpicuous, the Image, diamond shaped, of the Candle in it, especially, as it now appeared, I have emptied the Snuffers into it, & the Snuff floating about, & painting all-shaped Shadows on the bottom.' The poor wretch is in urgent need of counselling.

Concerning the delight he had in visiting the houses of English noblemen, Ruskin remarked that, as soon as he could perceive any political truth at all, it struck him as 'probably much happier to live in a small house and have Warwick Castle to be astonished at, than to live in Warwick Castle and have nothing to be astonished at'. He went on to say that, though he had received kind invitations to visit America, he couldn't live, even for a couple of months, in 'a country so miserable as to possess no castles'.

Goethe took the opposite view. 'America, you are better off than our old continent,' he wrote in a poem, 'You have no ruined castles . . .' The poem laments the burden of the past, the useless memories and futile wranglings which disturb one's living in the present (a fundamental Goethean thought), and which America was spared. It concludes with a sort of blessing on the New World:

> Use the present to happy effect!
> And your children, when they grow into poets,
> May a benevolent fate protect
> From stories of knights and robbers and spirits.

Fate was to prove benevolent in that respect, but not in some others.

Incidentally, Goethe told Eckermann in 1824 that he was glad not to be starting out at the present time, a time 'so thoroughly finished', when the young were terribly clever and there was so much competition. 'If I sought refuge in America, I should come too late, for there is now too much light even there.'

In his youth Ruskin never doubted a word of the Bible, but the more he believed it, the less good it did him. 'It was all very well for Abraham to do what angels bid him—so would I, if any angels bid me; but none had ever appeared to me that I knew of.' Many of us have suffered a similar deprivation. Ruskin admits that Adèle, the fifteen-year-old daughter of Mr Domecq, his father's partner in the sherry trade, would have fitted the job description, except she couldn't be an angel since she was a Roman Catholic.

Moral Tale

Poor Tasso, he doesn't have many visitors in prison,
He gets so lonely he's obliged to write dialogues.
But here's someone, if only a familiar spirit.
'Come and sit on the bed.' That posture, says the spirit,
Isn't easy for him. 'Let's just assume I'm sitting.'
Like other jailbirds, Tasso wants to talk about women,
And how they turn out so different from one's imaginings.
'Not their fault,' the spirit demurs. 'You ask too much
Of them. Or too little. Women are flesh and blood,
Like men, and you don't expect much of men, do you?'
But the poet yearns to see his beloved. 'Very well,
You shall dream of her this night,' the visitor avows.
It's the least a familiar can do. Tasso looks glum.
But dreams are richer than reality, his friend declares:
A man he knows, when he has met his mistress in a dream,
Is careful to avoid her on the morrow, lest he spoil it.
For 'Pleasure is always in the past or in the future,
Never in the present.' 'Ergo it doesn't exist,' says Tasso
Dolefully, and life's a wretched business, void of pleasure
And beset by ennui. 'What?' The spirit doesn't know the word.
Tasso explains. 'I get it,' says the other: 'Ennui
Is what human life is largely made of.' Tasso wonders
If there are remedies for it. Oh yes, the spirit tells him—
Sleep, opiates, and pain, and pain is the most effective.
'While a man is really suffering, he won't feel bored
At all.' Prison life is enervating, and perhaps Tasso
Is bored with suffering. His eyes keep closing. It's time
For the spirit to leave and arrange the promised dream.
'Do drop in again,' the poet mumbles. 'Where do you hang out?'
'Haven't you cottoned on yet? In any strong drink.'

        (after a dialogue of Leopardi's)

'GOD is no saint, strange to say. There is much to object to in him, and many attempts have been made to improve him': from *God: A Biography*, by Jack Miles, formerly a Jesuit, now a freelance journalist.

At a party I meet a Jesuit priest, a man of intellectual distinction and seemingly of amiable or simply urbane disposition. I daren't ask him whether he believes in God and God's goodness. Is it that I don't wish to embarrass him? Or that I don't want to embarrass myself? Would you ask a politician if he believed in politics, a mother if she believed in motherhood, a millionaire if he believed in money and its goodness?

Perhaps the question is embarrassing merely because it has long been established that (a) God exists and (b) God does not exist, and everything that can be said, both under (a) and under (b), has been said over and over again. (Just as it is easier to chat about the merits or demerits of a new novel than exchange views on *Little Dorrit* or *Tom Jones*.) So what I talk about with the priest is the work of a Catholic mission in Zaïre, and then, slightly more daringly, the fuss about female ordination in the other Church.

I suppose the truth is, I am feeble. Unlike the priest, I suspect, who gives the impression of being willing to embark on any subject whatsoever, cloth or no cloth. (In fact he is in mufti.) He now reflects on the death from AIDS of the mutual friend whose memorial service we have just attended, whose wake this is. Here is the moment I could put my question about believing in God. But I don't. He offers me a plate of canapés.

I recall an aphorism attributed to Sir Arthur Helps, a trusted adviser to Queen Victoria, who died of pleurisy after catching cold while attending a levee. 'Never make a god of your religion.' Or you could say, Never make a religion of your god. Strange to say, there may be much to object to in him.

The guilt felt in age—there being more time for it—concerning those things done, these things not done; omissions hurting more than commissions, supposing you can tell one from the other.

> Now I am here, what thou wilt do with me
> None of my books will show:
> I read, and sigh, and wish I were a tree;
> For sure then I should grow
> To fruit or shade: at least some bird would trust
> Her household to me, and I should be just.

George Herbert died before his fortieth birthday. His guilt was at least short-lived. He appears to have been virtually a saint. Touch wood.

Fauré's *Requiem*—it doesn't merely make you wish you were a Christian, it makes you feel you are one. (If I hear *Façade* one more time, I shall know I'm in hell.)

An entry in Amiel's *Journal*: 'Ah! when will the Church to which I belong in heart rise into being? I cannot content myself with being in the right all alone.'

'In the twentieth, as in the first century, we find the burden of Christianity borne by solitary and often anonymous individuals'; i.e. rather than by the Churches. Thus Hubert Butler, the Irish writer, in 1988.

One learns all sorts of things from one's pupils. In 1931 Butler was teaching in Leningrad, and that winter saw the fortieth anniversary of Gorky's début as a writer. Among other celebrations, a bomber plane was dedicated to him. A woman claimed that Gorky was a 'gumanist' (our 'h' is 'g' in Russian) and that a bomber would not please him very much. Butler asked his pupils to define 'gumanism'. A man said in English, 'It is what you say "namby-pamby".' The woman protested, and 'it appeared that about half the class thought nambi-pambiness a good thing'. The resident spy, keen to avoid trouble, proposed a return to the set text.

The outsider often entertains an unreal and rosy notion of the inside. Zeno, Italo Svevo's character, was of the opinion that his wife's religion took little time to acquire and less to put into practice. 'You bowed your knee and returned to ordinary life again immediately! That was all.' For him religion was a very different thing. 'If I had only believed, nothing else in the world would have mattered to me.' One doesn't have to be as accomplished a self-deceiver as Zeno to deceive oneself on this score.

❦

A JAPANESE artist is to create a work of art by tracing over ten days the movements of a solitary ant across an area of eight square metres in a London gallery. The gallery director explains that *Wandering Position*, as the work is to be called, 'invites analogies with the strategies of social control that exist within human society, and the troubling realities of limitation and restraint'. Quite a subject, and only one little ant to tackle it!

A spoilsport from the London Zoo insists that a solitary ant wouldn't be likely to survive the show, since without a true purpose in life ants give up the ghost. For an ant, art wouldn't constitute such a purpose. In the event the artist appears to have got round this obstacle by engaging a relay of ants.

It so happened that the day after spotting this news item ('make it new' now means 'make it news'), I had a phone call from a young woman at a California college. It seemed that her class were studying an old poem of mine and they weren't quite sure of its meaning, though they thought it had to do with war. I told her that the poem simply played on common or uncommon typing errors ('frontears', 'tygirl tygirl burning bride') and the various keys of a typewriter ('TAB e or not TAB e i.e. the ?'). Finally I pointed her to the brand of machine I had used at the time: a 'Swetish Maid' called—

I began to stammer: one never knows whether Americans are sophisticated in the extreme or not at all—called 'Facit'. In short, the poem didn't really mean more than it failed to say.

'Oh,' she said, with only the faintest tinge of disenchantment, 'we were told that in the 1960s you were a foreign correspondent in Southeast Asia, and so . . .' I apologized: in the 1960s I was merely foreign. As for the poem, it was just—I forced the expression out—just a fun poem. 'Well, thank you, sir,' she said, polite to the end.

Some people write better than they know, others worse.

Exhibited elsewhere, and making news, is the creation of a young British artist: a statue of the Virgin Mary encased in a condom. This piece of symbolism—high-powered although standing only three inches high—is in acute need of what proves a long and tedious explication. The artist desires to place the Virgin in the context of her—the artist's—'concerns about issues of sexuality, contraception, safe-sex messages in the community, and abortion'. No disrespect is intended to the mother of Jesus, but the Pope will be shaking in his shoes.

The head of the Li Family deployed eight rows of dancers in the ceremonies at his ancestral temple. Confucius commented: 'If he is capable of that, what will he not be capable of?'

In his translation of the *Analects* Simon Leys observes that only the ruler was entitled to eight rows of dancers, and the gentleman in question had a right to four. This usurpation of royal privileges strengthened Confucius's sense of witnessing the crumbling of civilization.

A celebrated theatre director reminds us that among other things he has made a number of plays. These plays—which, in ordinary English, he has staged—were written or made, as far as we know, by a number of insignificant persons including a W. Shakespeare.

A living dog isn't merely better than a dead lion; it's better than a living lion. Just as a dead cow in formaldehyde is better than a living cow in a field.

A smart parenthesis of Roland Barthes's: '(in Japan, some Frenchmen dislike removing their shoes, either for fear of losing their virility or because they are embarrassed at the hole in their stocking)'. (Or because it's an ungainly operation, painfully highlighted by the dexterity shown by the natives. Or because—at the beginning of a party, say—it makes you feel you are being sent to bed. Or because you're not as keen on bathing as your hosts.)

This welcome diversion pops up in the middle of an excruciatingly perverse 'reading' (dread word) of the Marquis de Sade, of a depth, intensity and ingenuity never bestowed on Dickens, George Eliot, etc. For example: 'The language of debauchery is often *beaten out*. It is a Cornelian, Caesarian language: "'My friend,' I said to the youth, 'you see all I have done for you; it is high time to recompense me.' 'What is it you want?' 'Your ass.'" . . .'

Samuel Garth achieved fame with *The Dispensary* (1699), which dealt with the high price of medicines and the inability of the poor to afford them. Dr Johnson reported that 'The poem, as its subject was present and popular, co-operated with passions and prejudices then prevalent, and, with such auxiliaries to its intrinsic merit, was universally and liberally applauded.' Garth's later reputation, or lack of it, he summed up thus: the work 'appears to want something of poetical ardour, and something of general delectation; and therefore, since it has been no longer supported by accidental and extrinsic popularity, it has been scarcely able to support itself'. I fear the like will be said before long, if anything at all is said, of many of today's universally and liberally applauded artistic productions.

In connection with Kafka's 'Josephine the Singer', J. P. Stern has remarked on 'the vast excess, in works of art, of effort and wrought artefact over the effect noticed and understood, let alone appreciated by the public at large'. (The same might be said of other things, for instance one's wife's cooking.) Think, on the other hand, of those successful books to all appearances produced by a computer happily unacquainted with the concepts of effort and artefact. A line may take us hours, said Yeats in a poem, but if it doesn't seem a moment's thought then all our stitching and unstitching amounts to nothing. In this case, wouldn't a moment's thought be more effective, since it is bound to seem more like a moment's thought? — and moreover would spare us that vast and profligate excess noted above.

Yeats's poem, by the way, is entitled 'Adam's Curse'. Adam had a singularly small public to notice, understand and possibly appreciate his work.

From the sparse prose of Paul Celan, Jewish German-language poet.

Replying to a questionnaire about writers' work in progress, 1958: 'But am I anywhere near your question yet? Those poets! One ends up wishing that, one day, they might manage to get a solid novel down on paper.'

Speech on receiving the Georg Büchner Prize, 1960: '. . . quotation marks, which perhaps we shouldn't call goose feet [*Gänsefüsschen*], but rather rabbits' ears, that is, something which listens, not without fear, for something beyond itself, beyond words'.

Speech on receiving the Bremen Literature Prize, 1958; a neat way of conveying both gratitude and reproach, summoning up both what is shared and what wasn't (his parents died in a Nazi camp): 'Thinking [*denken*] and thanking [*danken*] are words having the same roots in our language. If we follow it through, we enter the semantic field of recollect [*gedenken*], bear in mind [*eingedenk sein*], remembrance [*Andenken*] and devotion [*Andacht*]. Permit me, from this standpoint, to thank you.'

ONE of the old school. Our headmaster, Mr Arnold Thornton, would remind us during assembly that his initials stood for Até, a god who wreaked vengeance on those miserable creatures unable to tell right from wrong. This announcement, repeated at regular intervals, was accompanied by a smile at once benign and minatory. It made us shiver. We loved it.

Life had its peculiar pleasures in those days. There was no call to spray graffiti on the lavatory walls, or rob a sweetshop, or stab a teacher. There was the delicious qualm felt on hearing that the Physics master, a Welshman, literally had eyes in the back of his head, that sticking a stamp on an envelope with the monarch's head upside down amounted to high treason and could get you put in the Tower, or (not so delicious) that a person called a bayleaf would take your furniture away if the rent-book wasn't kept up to date.

I suppose that most of us at the school were accustomed to neatly sliced squares of newspaper kept in the lavatory at home. It was an everyday matter, taken for granted. Then one day, in the woodwork class when at last we were allowed to make what we chose instead of rudimentary shapes, a classmate came up with a simple box. The woodwork master—the most odious by far of all the teachers I've known—asked the boy what the box was intended for. Having been stammeringly informed, the master burst out in gloating contempt: so the boy's family wiped themselves with old newspapers, a filthy habit, you could catch a nasty disease, hadn't they heard of toilet paper . . . The boy stood silent, his face red, not far from tears. The rest of us remained silent too; our bums began to itch.

This incident came to mind when I was reading Alan Bennett's *Writing Home*, where he notes that in hotels these days the ends of toilet rolls are often plaited. (Presumably to demonstrate that no one has been there before you.) Luckily they didn't do this when he was a child, or he would have thought his family's toilet roll was unique— disgracefully so—in its 'ragged and inconsequent termination'. At least his family had toilet rolls. But there's always some way that people can put you to shame.

Do you eat asparagus with your fingers, or use a fork? Either way someone will judge you uncouth. Pronounce the word 'vallet' rather than 'vallay' and most people will think you unlettered. Others will smile on you, among them those who employ a valet.

Maeve Binchy, Irish novelist, has told how, after her first night in a hotel, she didn't know whether to make the bed or not. A perfectly understandable quandary for anyone not used to being waited on. Like any benighted, intelligent person, in the end she half-made it.

In *Unholy Pleasure, or The Idea of Social Class*, P. N. Furbank mentions a Swiss tax group who will dance only with one another. (My current tax status might make it hard to find a presentable partner.) Apropos of supposed economic bonds, Furbank observes that while, for all we know, Iris Murdoch may enjoy the same income as the Lord Mayor of Bristol, 'this does not create a bond between them'. Yet one would love to see the distinguished novelist and the civic dignitary quickstepping together across the Clifton suspension bridge.

'The old orphan attitudes—he who is kept out tries both to stay out and to get in': Karl Miller, *Rebecca's Vest*. Yes, but usually one more doggedly than the other, whatever the attendant compunctions and misgivings.

Class haiku

All very well, 'the
Station in which one was born'—
So few trains leaving!

Outing. No, not a school trip to nearby Bournville to see chocolate being made or to the boring factory where they turned out varicoloured building blocks for babies. (Both gave us free samples of their products.) Homosexuals are now expected—or induced—to declare themselves. (Coming out is one thing, though not necessarily of widespread concern; being forced out is another.) Were heterosexuals ever expected to declare themselves? (Yes, behind the bicycle sheds or in the public bar.) I remember when one strove to conceal the fact that one was sexual in any sense or direction.

At least in those days there were discoveries to be made on the quiet. I don't mean discovering that some politician or bishop or actor was homosexual. Or, come to that, heterosexual. There was something to be said (or there is something to be said in retrospect) for covering up the legs of pianos.

Leamington College for Boys vanished years ago. And now the old playing-field—scene of so many trouncings of our First Fifteen by other schools' Second Fifteens—accommodates a small, faintly upmarket housing estate. The problem was to find names for the streets. What about College Old Boys? The only famous one, Sir Frank Whittle, inventor of the jet engine, was already commemorated elsewhere in the town. Well, there was Lytton Strachey, who spent three years there: unhappy to begin with, nicknamed 'Scraggs', and bullied, but reconciling himself a trifle superciliously to what in the 1890s, obviously at its zenith, was a 'semi-demi public school'. In 1937 a school house was named after him.

My sister takes me to view Enright Close, a cramped opening between houses, dominated by a large sign: DEAD END.

ONE of the 'quality' Sunday papers has a supplement called 'Real Life'. It consists largely of the serial liaisons of famous people one has never heard of, fashionable restaurants here and abroad, fashion models of all sexes, the egos of meandering columnists, trendy agony aunts ('My boyfriend keeps biting me really quite hard when we have sex. I find it really annoying and off-putting'), advice on the pros and cons of letting your bra strap show, on how to conquer your cellulite, and how to pick up someone in the Underground, advice to a Muslim male, forbidden to wear silk, on tracking down cotton ties that aren't flowery or common, articles headed 'The intelligent consumer' (on, for instance, the convenience of dreadlocks), 'Would you let a gay man look after your child?' (answer: yes, because a 'straight' male nanny would be suspect), 'I live in a *ménage-à-trois*' (not highly recommended), and 'I fell in love with a gay man' (the 'I' being female, and in two minds about it), a whole page on—what a coup!—the joy of not having sex (Madonna would rather read a book, Edwina Currie writes books instead).

Does this imply that the rest of the paper is unreal? No, not exactly unreal; just not very pertinent or true to real life.

Sunday: once a holy day, suffocatingly dull, bullied by bells, everything closed except churches. It prepared us for returning, with some readiness, to school or work on Monday.

Sunday: now the most exciting day, everything open, celebrated by newspapers starring varieties of sexual experience, drugs, murders, food and drink, alluring holiday offers. It spoils one for returning to work or school on Monday.

But we need to cram our Sundays full somehow. In 1870 Amiel declared that the efficacy of religion lay not in the rational, philosophic or eternal, but precisely in the unforeseen, the miraculous, the extraordinary. 'In our day, those who wish to get rid of the supernatural, to enlighten religion, to economize faith, find themselves deserted, like poets who should declaim against poetry, or women who should decry love.'

Hence the passion in our own day for the paranormal (a more respectable concept than the supernatural), as evinced by at least three television series running concurrently, on top of UFO stories and science fiction and fantasy. The supernatural has gone down-market; religion has gone out of the market.

※

HUMOUR, humorous: cognate with 'humid', from Latin *humor*, moisture. 'Often allied to pathos,' says the dictionary. One's eyes are moist, rarely with tears of mirth, one laughs so as not to cry. The famous clown with the breaking heart, *lacrimae rerum*, politically wet (cf. dry eyes), Hardy's 'long drip of human tears', tears not idle enough, Blake's 'intellectual things'. Also crocodile's, mourning over its meal.

And of course the old humours, bodily fluids governing the temperament, sanguine, phlegmatic, choleric, melancholic; hence the unfunny comedy of psychosis. An early version of genes; Johnson confessed, 'I inherited a vile melancholy from my father.'

All in all, scarcely a laughing matter.

Two old jokes, amusing in their time, which have lost their savour and their sense. (1) Finding his young son in the hayloft with a milkmaid, the farmer berates him: 'Next you'll be smoking!' (2) A woman writes to an agony aunt: 'Dear Jane, I have just discovered that my husband is heterosexual. What shall I do?'

Plans are in hand to raise the minimum age for the buying of cigarettes from 16 to 18, and simultaneously to lower the age of consent for homosexuals from 18 to 16.

The best spoof is the one you can't be sure is a spoof. Umberto Eco's 'Three Owls on a Chest of Drawers' is an analysis of diversely methodological analyses of an intriguing Italian sestina. Among the assembled scholars are Harold Bloom, Stanley Fish, Jacques Lacan, Jacques Derrida (his unfinished paper, 'Limited Ink'), and the less well-known Chafe, Chafe, and Chafe, 1978. On Lacan's 'justly famous Séminaire XXXV', a note advises, 'For better comprehension I refer to the Urdu translation.' We gather that for Lacan the chest of drawers 'is in fact the place of repression', and 'the pulsatile action' of the owls (who in the sestina are making love with the daughter of a doctor) is 'only apparently inspired by desire', and to be interpreted as a disguise of the *Bemächtigungsstreich*: 'or rather, as Lacan himself clarified in his limpid French, an *Überwältigung* of the girl object'.

That this is all spoofery is suggested only by the publishers listed in the bibliography. Getting Even Press, 1992; Owlish Press, n.d., Donald Duckworth, 1999. And even so one can't be absolutely sure.

Amiel Abstracted

All I care for is
The serious. Me I can't
Take seriously.

❧

THE art of the headline in periodical reviewing. On the whole editors seem to prefer bland, inexpressive titles—perhaps nice-mindedly wishing not to pre-empt or upstage what the reviewer has to say. But at times one comes across something catchy, such as 'Strange bedfellows' for a piece on professional gardeners and their relations with clients, and 'Auto biography' for a series on the history and mystique of makes of cars (both in *Independent on Sunday*). From the *Times Literary Supplement*: 'Bile with style', a review of a choleric Austrian writer, and 'Look on't again I dare not', of a dreadful production of *Macbeth*. A review in *The Spectator* of a book on bottoms was headed 'The end justifies the jeans', and an account in *The Times* of a production of *Mahagonny*: 'Weill bodies'.

'A slice of American apple-piety' (a sweet or sentimental novel about two young boys, *Guardian*), 'The school of hard knocks' (a book on the materials used by sculptors, *London Review of Books*), 'Nerd-World leaders' (about the Microsoft phenomenon and Internet hype, *TLS*), 'Les Filles de Joe' (Joe having had lots of girlfriends, *The Oldie*) — these are a mite contrived, but not without appeal.

I've always supplied headings, as a point of paltry honour; sometimes they have been kept, more often not. Possibly a point of editorial honour is involved. *The Spectator* kept 'Variegations on a theme', to do with a study of the primary colours and their connotations, but dropped 'Eheu!' for a collection of tributes to the late publisher and classicist, Colin Haycraft, in favour of 'Publish and be praised': an improvement.

You have to have headings, and in large type; but does anyone register them?

※

'DE Trois Commerces': Montaigne's approach to feminism. Women shouldn't seek to be learned, they possess natural riches enough, they have the whip hand where it counts. Why should they stifle their own brilliance merely to shine with a borrowed light? 'Quid ultra? Concumbunt docte': What's more, you find yourself sleeping with an egghead (Juvenal). If women insist on book-learning, then let it be poetry, an art playful and subtle, veiled, verbal, all pleasure and all appearance, like themselves.

So it looks as though the men who put them up to all this learning did so in order to put them down.

'Women's erotic fiction has done brilliantly. Black Lace novels, unhampered by problems with models, erections ("you can find many erect penises in Black Lace" assures the publicity blurb) or being on the top shelf, started in 1993 and have sold 1.5 million copies, representing half of the total market share.' (*Independent on Sunday*, 1996.)

What's sauce for the gander is sauce for the goose; we wouldn't want any élitism around. Good that there's no evidence of erection-envy.

A more general comment of Karl Kraus's comes to mind. 'And the advocates of women's rights? Instead of fighting for the woman's natural rights, they get all fired up about the woman's obligation to behave unnaturally.' (1908.)

A friend in Australia reports that a woman has proposed a 'testosterone tax' on males, in that 95 per cent of prisoners in the country are men and custody costs £25,000 per annum per prisoner, so why should women be expected to contribute towards the expense? Ours is an age of teeming new ideas, chiefly old grievances. Am I my brother's keeper?

We banged on about the 'contemporary relevance' of great literature, and look what's happened. Someone has just declared, 'The key to Lear is that he is, in a sense, a single parent.'

A friend, a university lecturer in English, has come across this in an essay by one of her students on a much admired poet: 'The body of her poetry is very sparingly marked by the signs of imperialistic and patriarchal tradition such as commas and periods.' One can just about detect the point: women have traditionally been kept within commas, hurtfully hyphenated, confined inside brackets, and subject to full stops. In this case subject to imperialism as well, the poet having been born in British Guiana. But 'What have I done?' asks my friend.

(Just a little more ingeniously, it could be proposed that, in a sense, Lear is an elderly, outmoded arts journalist, trodden down by the hungry generations of youth, but putting a brave face on it: noting who loses and who wins, who's in, who's out, taking upon himself the mystery of things, as if he were God's spy, and wearing out packs and sects of great ones who ebb and flow by the moon.)

Camille Paglia admires gay men for their 'fusion of intellect, emotion, and artistic sensibility'. 'They are born with an artistic gene,' she says. 'The intellectual of the twenty-first century, trained by an academic system I am trying to reshape, will think like a gay man.'

It sounds much like the view common when (and where) I was growing up—that fellows interested in books, music, art, were nancy boys. (In fact some of those I knew were homosexual, others were emphatically heterosexual, though it was only later that I realized this; at the time I saw them as congenial individuals interested in books, music, art.) Once artistic men were homosexual; now homosexual men are artistic.

One good thing about Camille Paglia is that she likes women and thinks well of them. They need men—it's their destiny to rule them.

Also she likes literature and thinks well of it. 'James Joyce's *Ulysses* does what Foucault claims to be doing but never gets around to. The points Foucault makes about insanity and normality, my God, all these points have been raised from Blake onwards.' It's a queer business, that artistic gene.

'Let men take their choice. Man and woman were made for each other, though not to become one being; and if they will not improve women, they will deprave them': Mary Wollstonecraft, 1792.

In *Wilhelm Meister's Apprenticeship*, the eccentric Harper defends incest by adducing the lilies: 'Do not husband and wife spring from the same stem?' Mignon—the Harper's daughter by his sister, it turns out—is both a girl and a boy, or a girl who insists on being considered a boy (but none the less falls in love with Wilhelm). On one occasion, in that endearing way he sometimes has of not being quite certain of his characters, Goethe alludes to Mignon as 'it'.

Primitive forms of life are undifferentiated sexually, or combine both sexes. We have seen periods in which the sexes were sharply differentiated ('Me Tarzan—you Jane'), too radically according to recent thought. Now we seem to be reverting to that more primitive condition: unisex, bisexuality, 'grey areas' of indistinctness and uncertainty. As if life is collapsing back into itself, returning to its origins. Maybe the end of the world *is* nigh, as nigh goes in these matters.

How bracing to listen in on Djuna Barnes interviewing the American actress, Lillian Russell, in May 1914.

'Well, then, don't you think at least something is going to the dogs, Miss Russell—surely some one thing?'

'I can't think of a single thing. Let me see—with women in the world how can things go to the dogs.'

It would be pettifogging to submit that some things were soon to go to the dogs, the dogs of war. But it does seem prudent, though a pity, to bring in Mary Wollstonecraft again: 'When therefore I call women slaves, I mean in a political and civil sense; for indirectly they obtain too much power, and are debased by their exertions to obtain illicit sway.'

Best of all (one can breathe again), Hélène Cixous: 'I regret not being Tiresias . . . I am not Tiresias. I am not God. I am only a woman, which is already a great deal . . . I'm also a human being.'

※

WE British don't go in much for explaining things to foreigners; either because we think they ought to know already, or because we fear explanations will have awkward consequences.

The Egyptians, as I found them, were always ready to expound and clarify. Once a party of us from the university in Alexandria were exploring the marvels of Luxor and Aswan. Trudging wearily through some village in Upper Egypt, we were approached by a hospitable elder who insisted that we should take our rest and witness yet another marvel: an exhibition of belly-dancing, about to begin on an improvised stage. The plank benches were crammed with a multitude of impatient men, but the elder gave orders and an extra bench was set in front for us, very close to the stage. The women in our party were politely escorted from the scene.

The first turn was mild, even genteel, a curtain-raiser. As soon as the real and barely credible thing began, the whole audience swayed back and forth with an ever-growing momentum and creaking of benches, in rhythm with heavy appreciative breathing. 'Christ!' said a colleague, an Englishman, sitting next to me, 'We'll be crushed!' But then a young fellow from the back leapt on the stage and flung himself at the dancer. At once a mass of country policemen, without uniforms but bearing long staffs, appeared from both sides, beat the impetuous fellow with energetic gestures but little force, and hustled him away. A communal 'Ah!' arose from the audience, a release of pent-up feelings or perhaps relief that they had escaped whipping.

A young villager who had seated himself beside me, turned and said solemnly, 'Sar, he wants to love her very much, but they will not let him.' It couldn't have been put more lucidly.

She complains. They stole away her mother tongue. She cannot write for her mother, her grandmother. They imposed a foreign language on her, reaching a huge public, but cluttered with famous dead or half-dead white male authors, bullying father figures. How did that American put it? '. . . imperialist and colonialist appropriation of space . . . drives to power and mastery which require slavery as their correlative'. She's no slave. She'll choose alterity, and revel in *différance*! But she complains. Underneath one senses another grievance, unspoken. 'Why can't I be a better writer?' Join the club, Ms!

Judge not, that ye be not judged. True as it may be, it won't do to object that you'll be judged anyway.

In his *Journal* André Gide records how he and Dorothy Bussy, his English translator and Lytton Strachey's sister, were waiting for a train to Menton when they noticed a trio of 'foreigners' who were talking loudly and gobbling greedily from a large hold-all. 'Quelle vulgarité!' Then, to compound the horrors, one of the women, presumably the wife, took the man in her arms and, clucking the while, covered him in kisses. To Gide's amazement, the man seemed to shrink, and slipped through the woman's arms, his eyes rolling upwards, his mouth wide open. He had had a stroke.

Gide was indignant to see the wife still clutching a tartlet, strawberry or cherry, which she had been about to eat. Then he realized it was the man's denture, which had jumped from his mouth, and the wife was trying to replace it, her back turned decently to the company.

Poor people, good people, how could he have despised them! 'We should guard against heartless judgements: one risks taking a set of false teeth for a jam tart!'

A last spurt of anti-imperialist resentment in a country which gained independence forty years ago: it's okay to have 'Pomp and Circumstance March' in the concert programme, but the orchestra certainly may not play 'Land of Hope and Glory'.

Fine distinctions are sometimes quite appealing. There was a story they used to tell in Egypt, of how when Lord X arrived there as the new High Commissioner of the dependency, he was welcomed warmly by local notables: a good, wise man, a true friend of Egypt, utterly unlike the detested Sir Y Y ('hear! hear!'), who had served in a similar capacity several years earlier . . .

Sir Y Y had in the interval been raised to the peerage as Lord X.

An exhibition of old colonial postcards

Street Scenes from the 1890s. Exceedingly tidy.
There is nobody to be seen in the streets.

Here is the Padang. The Padang is still here.
'Cricket is played in the evenings.' It can't be evening.

And now the General Post Office. 'The most important P.O.
in the East,' said Joseph Conrad. A man is buying a stamp.

A succession of schools of all denominations or none.
Here they were taught language. And they profited.

Colourful washing strung across bustling Battery Road.
Or is it banners bearing ambiguous devices?

A world-famous old hotel, 'the hub of social life in the 1900s'.
The natives had no social life, they had families.

This is a Chinese funeral, 'suitably exotic'. Then a Malay one,
suitably simple, burial before sunset on the day of demise.

Central Police Station. Built by the Public Works in 1905, with
Islamic clock tower. 'Doleful shall be the fate of transgressors.'

The Chinese Recreation Club; not unlike a large bandstand.
They recreated themselves in their own peculiar manner.

Convent Chapel, French Gothic. The Convent houses a girls' school,
an orphanage, and a refuge for distressed women of all races.

The Quays are lined with the godowns of taipans and towkays.
The Wharves are crowded with busy dwarves.

The Jungle 1910. Lush in appearance, in fact infertile.
'Only the Chinese gambler throve.' Sorry, the Chinese gambier.

Malay Kampong Life. If there are no schools in sight
it was so they could be educated as farmers and fishermen.

Regatta. Seen as a means of promoting racial harmony.
Every community took part, the Malays won all the boat races.

Coronation Day 1901. Edward VII's head is already on a stamp.
Two loyal natives attend in London, a lawyer and a physician.

Street Opera. Stage knocked up out of attap and bamboo.
Extremely noisy. Opera was a cure for homesickness.

Opium smoking 1900. See, everyone is smiling. The tycoons are happy that opium is taxed instead of their profits.

Hongkong & Shanghai Bank 1892. Cross between opera house and cathedral. Known to local Chinese as 'Abundance of Remittances'.

Beauties of the East 1905, when men outnumbered women eight to one. A tourist has scrawled, 'If these are beauties Lord help the ugly ones'.

H. N. 'Mad' Ridley with a Rubber Tree 1910. This is the great man who conceived a method of tapping latex without killing the tree.

Grandma's Joy 1900. A row of impassive children. Child mortality was 345 per thousand. Which is why they were called joys.

Chinese Protectorate 1900. Has a religious air. Concerned with the slave trade, prostitution, secret societies, and other good causes.

Bullock Cart. 'A clumsy and inefficient vehicle, yet essential while awaiting motorization.' The bullocks await patiently.

Teutonia Club. Founded by the German community 1856. Seized in 1914 as enemy property. Became a hotel in 1929. Used as residence for Japanese officers 1942–5. Then as War Crimes Trial Court. Currently Goodwood Park Hotel, fairly famous.

Botanic Gardens. 'Mad' Ridley, having invented rubber, invented orchids. The famous monkeys got above themselves and were weeded out in 1980.

Chinese Coolies unloading cargo. It is warm work. The word is Tamil for 'hireling'. Their descendants will have to import coolies.

St Andrew's Cathedral. Anglican, neo-Gothic, built in 1860 by Major McNair and convict labour. Now a National Monument.

This was the Oriental Hotel, also world-famous. Nowadays it is the Japanese Commercial Museum.

Amber Mansions, picturesque shops selling aspirin and snake wine. Demolished 1980s to make way for Mass Rapid Transit system.

Government House, where British Governor lived for a hundred years. Government continues. Now residence of President of the Republic.

Outside the museum are towerblocks and skyscrapers, all built by the natives, who live or work in them. They have forgotten they were natives.

※

'ADVERTISEMENTS are now so numerous that they are very negligently perused, and it is therefore become necessary to gain attention by magnificence of promises': Dr Johnson.

Michael Aspel, television celebrity, invites self and wife personally to an exclusive all-day champagne reception ('not advertised to the general public') in New Malden ('very easy to find'), at the DFS Upholstered Furniture Supercentre. The host is his friend, Sir Graham Kirkham, chairman of DFS.

Most kind of you, Mr Aspel. Unfortunately we are unable to avail ourselves of your champagne, your supercentre, and your five years' free credit. I have a prior engagement that day with an old easy chair and a can of beer.

'Dear Mr Enright,
Do you keep searching for the best value washing up liquid?'
No, but perhaps I should.
The accompanying picture is of a smiling young woman standing at a kitchen sink. If this joint approach is meant to avoid sexism, it fails. The man chooses, the woman uses.

Who said you can't reconcile egalitarianism and élitism? Everyone gets a brochure, slipped into the daily papers, advertising a certain credit card. The brochure proclaims: 'Not everyone gets it.'

Yet another kind offer to fix me up with 'the right partner' or 'special relationship', this time by 'using a combination of personal selection and information technology'. More soberly worded than some. Interesting to see that in the questionnaire 'religious preference' comes bottom, well below the subject of smoking.

A letter arrives offering a free month's supply of 'the fantastic hormone DHEA', greeted by the highly respected medical journal, *Vanity Fair*, as 'the most broadly useful natural medicine in the battle to resist ageing'. DHEA can help to prevent 'Cardiovascular Disease, (the worlds biggest killer disease) Cancer, Ageing, Alzheimer's Disease and Impotence, whilst at the same time increasing Memory Retention, Sexual Vitality and much more'. (The envelope is addressed to my wife, but never mind.)

Perhaps the offer should be taken up along with the 'special relationship' held out above. One's confidence is impaired slightly by the return-slip at the foot of the page: 'Please send me one months supply of DHEA on a free trail basis.' Where might it lead us?

※

ONE of Heinrich Böll's best pieces is a review (1976) of a book called *Jesus Son of Man*. Theologians write for other theologians, rather as the Lowells talk only to Cabots (whether God takes a hand in the conversation is a different matter). 'For whom is religion there,' Böll asks, 'for whom is it being processed by theology, if not for vulgus or populus?' Come to that, 'for what other purpose than to be vulgarized have theology, church, and religion ever existed?' You could also ask, what does 'Son of Man' really signify?

Böll, a cradle-Catholic, notes that the infallibility of the Pope, though an article of faith, meant no more to his grandmother than the man in the moon, and the mortal sin of adultery probably lay beyond her imagination. What she did take seriously was the requirement that Holy Communion should be received on an empty stomach; hence the anxious hours given to the possibility of a drop of water slipping down one's throat during the brushing of one's teeth. (Some of us may have experienced a similar if lesser anxiety in advance of a general anaesthetic.) In official circles this contingency is now regarded as laughably trivial, and Böll wonders which rules will be found equally trivial in the future—celibacy, birth control, the indissolubility of marriage?

On the theologians' distaste for poetry, of and for the vulgus, given to 'emotion', responsible for the historical unreliability of some text or other, Böll writes, 'Poetry is not equatable with falsehood, and legends and myths are not identical with lies.' Isn't it a most amazing miracle that faith 'has survived *despite* theology, and that there are still some vestiges of "church"?' (Cf. George Moore's sanguine witticism: 'The Church is divine. She even survives the clergy.') Böll speculates that one day it may turn out that the only theological and religious literature to be taken seriously is that written by poets.

'Vulgarization' doesn't mean dumping the poetry and bundling away the legends: far from it. Nor does it mean turning the Church into a fairground or a pop concert, or a receptacle for current 'relevances', or a Soviet-style rewriting body. Which isn't to say it shouldn't contain a strong humanist element: not shunting on to God everything that is contemptible (to borrow a phrase from Böll's Nobel lecture of 1973), not harrying people about that drop of water or even (God helps them that help themselves) that condom. Something useful for those theologians to try their hand at. Mustn't leave everything to the poets.

Otherwise, all efforts to trim its sails to the winds and wafts of change having failed, perhaps the Church should turn itself into a national-heritage quango. For instance, Disinterested Repository of Ancient Things, popularly known by its acronym.

In his Christmas message relayed to Asda supermarkets across the country, the Archbishop of Canterbury, punning on 'shoppers' and 'worshippers', jokes about the letter 'e' dropping out of 'Highest', whereby the angels proclaim, 'Glory to God in the High st'.

A rather splendid comment by a New York wit is recorded in Emerson's *Journals*: a certain clergyman 'was always looking about to see if there was not a vacancy in the Trinity'.

A former archbishop is praised as 'a not inappropriate prelate for his time'. Would he had been a not appropriate one.

The charge has it that some employers behave towards their employees like tin gods.
 Can the clergy rightfully join a trade union? The Church dissents, on the grounds that they are employees not of the Church but of God. There's no bargaining with him. Least of all when the union proposed bears the title Manufacturing, Science and Finance. (Presumption, Forbidden Knowledge, Mammon.) In any case, as the Prayer Book states, God's service is perfect freedom. And—a barely concealed threat?—the poet most conversant in these matters has pointed out that God really doesn't need men's work since thousands of angels speed at his bidding without rest, paid holidays or occupational pensions.

❦

IN his dualism of mind and body, Descartes may have overprized the former a little, but he was nearer the mark than the modern savants who consider the mind a vassal of the body—a body-servant—solely there to further the body's interests and keep it in good working order.
 The mind (once also known as soul, latterly as brain) serving and preserving the body? ('I think, therefore he is.') Humbly tendering

such counsels as 'Look before you leap', 'He who rides on a tiger can never dismount', and such pep talk as 'Every day, in every way, you are getting better and better'? The mind can be a good servant on occasion; it can be a bad schoolmaster, too. It places the body in diverse forms of peril, ranging from nervous convulsions to broken limbs, penury, prison and torture chamber. It's only in age that the body really gets to be boss, through the strength of weakness, leaving the mind gibbering impotently. Till at last they make friends, of a sort, fading in each other's arms.

A more drastic polarity, with the master-servant relationship reversed, occurs in Donne's 'The First Anniversary', which submits that the soul is conceived when we are born, but born only when we die:

> For though the soul of man
> Be got when man is made, 'tis born but then
> When man doth die. Our body's as the womb,
> And, as a midwife, death directs it home.

The annulment of morality, one might think (though one doubts Donne did), since the unborn soul, passive, cannot be responsible for the actions of the body. Or moral responsibility moves to the body in some sense, in that the servant-body, affected by a quasi-maternal instinct during a pregnancy of uncertain duration, would or should behave in such a fashion as not to jeopardize the foetus, and thereby add to 'that sin', elsewhere in Donne, 'where I begun,/Which is my sin, though it were done before'.

Whichever way you see the relationship, it appears to ask an awful lot of the two partners.

Mind, brain and (for the sake of argument) soul: are they coterminous? A simple theory, I gather, has it that the brain exists for the sake of sex—i.e. to help genes reproduce themselves—and so, therefore, does the mind.

Donne's sermon preached on New Year's Day 1625 contains a fierce passage of theodicy. His argument is, as it must be, the old one: God moves in a mysterious way, and the mystery is not for us to investigate. God emerges as a common enough type of dictator, if uncommonly long-term, or institutionalized terrorist. Our minds unenlightened, all we perceive is the short-term outcome. Ours not to reason why. *Why* is 'a dangerous and infectious monosyllable'. ('An execrable and damnable monosyllable' was Luther's more vehement expression.) 'It exasperates God,' Donne declaims, 'it ruins us.' But we go on asking *why*: it seems to be in our nature to do so. We are ruined because it exasperates God? Never mind all the talk of mercifulness, which some of us may not deserve or expect: God is lacking in rudimentary understanding of his own creation. (Ah, but haven't you forgotten 'that sin where I begun'?: nature is no excuse.)

Unending exasperation ('provocation' it's called these days) and unending ruination—the transaction has gone on ever since that incident in the Garden of Eden. Talmudists say it was at the twelfth hour of their sojourn there that our first parents were expelled, as early as that. God can move fast on occasion.

No mention of Christ in that sermon, the one unmysterious way. This is Donne the preacher, not Donne the poet, or the man.

Donne can indeed 'go too far', as Singapore students were wont to complain of anything offending their sense of decent moderation. (Claudius was deemed to have done this: 'Though the last king has died but two months ago, he has already married his widow and stopped all mourning. This is surely against court etiquette.' As Confucius might well have said.) According to another of Donne's sermons: 'As he that travels weary and late towards a great city, is glad when he comes to a place of execution . . .' Excuse me? Because, you see, the traveller then knows he is approaching the town. Similarly, 'when thou comest to the gate of death, be glad of that, for it is but one step from that to thy Jerusalem.'

A case of the analogue being less familiar than the analogized, and the moral needing to cast light on the parable. One might object— were one given to carping—that the traveller is nearing a well-appointed inn, whereas the 'thou' is about to die. More relishable is Montaigne's anecdote about the man who was to be hanged; when the attendant priest promised him he would sup that day with Our Lord, the man replied: 'You go, then. I'm fasting.'

The sermon was preached before the Prince Palatine and his wife, daughter of James I, and Donne had celebrated their marriage with an epithalamium six years earlier. The preacher announced: 'The sun is setting on thee, and that for ever . . . thy titles and offices, thy wife and children are departing from thee, and that for ever.' The Prince may have felt that Donne was going too far.

❧

A VERSE from the mid-seventeenth century begins piously (and as if to put the Psalmist right when he says, 'O Lord, make haste to save me'):

> God, whom no time confines, oft stays, to save
> Till hope and help, from all things else, are fled.

God may properly consider himself a last resort, stepping in only when his creatures have failed. The quatrain concludes:

> That so his work may the more glory have
> Christ did not come, till Lazarus was dead.

But does God suffer from a nagging sense of inadequacy, that he should feel it necessary to stand around flexing his muscles? Here Christ is made to sound like a laggardly paramedic.

When part of the church roof fell in on her head, Margery Kempe (early fifteenth-century workaday mystic) called out to Jesus for mercy. Before long her pains disappeared, and she was whole and well. Some of her neighbours saw this as a miracle, and magnified the Lord for preserving the woman. ('This creature' she commonly called herself: a becoming substitute for 'I' and 'me' in autobiographical writing.) Others saw the event in a quite different light, as a sign of wrath and vengeance against a pernicious female. They too magnified the Lord, but, since Margery hadn't been squashed flat, with less fervour.

God as metaphor . . . 'Vacant metaphors, eroded figures of speech, inhabit our vocabulary and grammar,' George Steiner says. 'They rattle about like old rags or ghosts in the attic.' Once, when I was on a flight from London to the Far East, we rose out of bright sunlight into a dark thundercloud. There was a loud jarring thud, and the plane lost height, the floor falling away from under us. 'This is your captain speaking': an engine had been knocked out by lightning, and we would have to dump fuel and return to Heathrow. The passengers took this news calmly, content to leave themselves in the hands of their captain. As if anticipating complaint and argument, the captain, suddenly petulant, added some ill-chosen words: 'There's nothing I can do about it, it's what's called an act of God.' The passengers took this less calmly, they fidgeted, they muttered to one another. (Could it be their next of kin had failed to pray hard enough for them?) This was no vacant metaphor. They weren't at all happy to hear that God was acting.

When a girl of seven has disappeared and is then found murdered, what is the mother to tell her other, younger daughter? The mother explains that Sophie has gone to heaven. Metaphors, whether vacant or not, have their uses; but they can lead to trouble. The little sister says, 'I want to go to heaven to be with Sophie.' What is the answer to that? Perhaps only, 'You'll have to wait.' Children are used to being told that. If she waits till she's older, she'll understand (if that's the right word) what happened to Sophie on earth.

The one being so pertinent these days and the other so outmoded, it is proposed that henceforth the Old Testament shall be known as the New Testament and the New as the Old.

A reader in Connecticut sends me an 'American counterpoint' to a captious verse entitled 'Decline of Theodicy'. *Absconditus*: out of sight, out of mind. My verse was a sort of 'God isn't'; this is headed 'God is':

> God is like Coke . . .
> He's the real thing.
>
> God is like Ford . . .
> He's got the better idea.
>
> God is like Gillette . . .
> He's the closest thing to you yet.
>
> God is like Reader's Digest . . .
> He's always renewable.
>
> God is like Cream of Wheat . . .
> He sticks with you.
>
> God is like Bayer Aspirin . . .
> He works wonders.
>
> God is like Right Guard . . .
> He gives you 24-hour protection.
>
> God is like Pan-Am . . .
> He makes the going great,

and so forth. My correspondent says he copied it from a sheet on the wall in a Jesuit retreat house in Ohio. When a religion is no longer allowed drownings, beheadings and burnings at the stake, it will require the services of a truly smart PRO.

Having demolished the theoretical proofs of God's existence, Kant perceived that his servant, old Lampe, couldn't be happy without God, and since man was meant to be happy, then practically speaking God had better exist. Heine concluded that Kant acted with almost as much wisdom as a friend of his, who broke all the lights on Weender Street in Göttingen and then, standing in the dark, made a lengthy speech about the practical necessity of street-lights, 'which he had broken only theoretically, in order to prove that we could see nothing without them'.

Visible signs

The nearby church I know only as a polling-station;
The mosque, hidden behind the trees, I only know
From one brief visit, chivvying the wary imam
For news of miracles in Islam. ('There are none.')
Which leaves the trees and the busy moving birds.
Scoff if you will at symbols. Where there are none,
There can't be very much worth symbolizing.

O suburban Britain, how blank you can be!
Coldly you allocate a street name, number, postcode,
Simply forbidding us to kill our neighbours
Or speak to them without sufficient cause.
It's good to be that Polish poet, and perceive
That 'signs must be human', and one should marvel
At that miracle, a man. Yet one might like a holy statue
To lift its unpolitical hand just once in a while.

If I told my neighbours, 'We must love one another or—',
I would die of shame. Or else they would kill me.
But I pat their various pets with furtive pleasure,
Asking their names of those whose names I never ask.
Across from the mosque a cat prepares for a greeting;
Beside the church a puppy lifts a paw. Somehow it seems
We share in the animal creation. *Veni, Creator!*

A PHILOSOPHER in Voltaire's *Micromégas* explains why he has just quoted Aristotle in Greek: 'One should always cite what one understands least in the language one least understands.' A decent teacher worries none the less: 'To recommend what you yourself don't understand can be embarrassing.' (David Ellis, *Wordsworth, Freud and the spots of time*.)

An unnamed teacher of a 'core' three-year course on literary theory for undergraduates describes his procedure: 'I will take Macherey in the third year as my example . . . he was introduced on the back of Althusser, on the back of quite a substantial knowledge of Marxist writing on history, some encounter with the Frankfurt School, but he was not introduced on the back of any knowledge of Freud or Lacan. The question that dramatically posed itself was do you stop after you've introduced Macherey and say "Okay, now to understand Macherey we need to go back to Freud, from Freud to Lacan and then we arrive back at Macherey all in due course"? In the end there wasn't time to do that . . . So we tried to get round the problem by making our study of Macherey dependent on his Althusserian co-ordinate and setting aside any detailed engagement with Freud and Lacan.'

One sees that three years wouldn't be time enough for all those two-backed beasts. Another teacher observes fretfully that his students 'get very annoyed with you . . . and say "you're just making this up and this is ridiculous and why can't we just read the text without any of this theory?" Some students don't like it at all, they're here because they're successful. What are they successful at? Talking about Shakespeare's characters. They can do that and get an A, why should they bother what I say?'

A good question. They thought they were going to read English.

Which reminds me of something that happened in the 1970s. The publishing staff were away on the annual outing, and I was alone in the building, intending to visit my wife, in hospital, in the late afternoon. Suddenly there irrupted an agitated, dishevelled figure, gabbling in French. He was Jacques Lacan. It seemed we were publishing a book of his, with an introduction by another distinguished author on our psychoanalytical list, and M. Lacan had got it into his head, with (I imagine) scant reason, that the introducer would misrepresent him and, in ways I obviously wasn't going to appreciate, traduce him. This, I told him, was well outside my field, and malheureusement the editor responsible for our more arcane publications was away for the day. I assured him that he was bound to see the introduction before the book went to the printer. My words had no effect. M. Lacan grew more and more distraught, his arms waving, sweat shooting from his brow. There I was, perusing a typescript on Austen or Trollope or maybe Shakespeare, when (in Milton's phrase) all hell broke loose. What should I do if he had a stroke? Eventually, making soothing noises, I edged him down the stairs and into William IV Street. 'Au revoir, Monsieur, prenez soin de vous . . .' After that I never missed any of the firm's outings.

Still, one had better take cognizance of the consolation, however pusillanimous, depicted in a verse by some squeamish Japanese *sensei* (i.e. teacher, respected master):

> Yet a preoccupation with the incomprehensible has its uses.
> It diverts one's attention from the wanton spitting
> And the waddling rat in the dried-up sluices.
>   In one's haste
> To keep pace with the higher realities, one fails
> To perceive the inferior quality of the saké.
>   Thus taste drives out taste.

THIS is a free world, and we don't expect to pay for our principles. A yacht named *Nicorette* (after an anti-smoking product, chewing-gum and patches) is most indignant at being excluded from a race sponsored by Rothmans, the tobacco firm.

A week or so later Rothmans realize, or are tipped off, that they have been guilty of discrimination. Accordingly they announce that *Nicorette* is to be admitted after all. A director denies that the change of heart is dictated by bad publicity, adding, 'We don't encourage people to smoke. Our business is to encourage people to switch brands.' I wonder if this abstemiousness is unique among advertisers. The passion for political correctness is bound to lead to duplicity, double-talk, Pharisaism, and other grave incorrectnesses.

I read that in Buenos Aires there is a statue of a famous guitarist with a lighted cigarette, ever replenished, between his lips. In other countries the plinth would bear an inscription: 'Smoking seriously damages health.' (Quite beside the point: the guitarist died in a plane crash.)

I promise myself: I shall in no circumstances sue the tobacco manufacturers, the makers of pipes, tobacco pouches, matches, or lighters.

Lawsuits are all the rage. Someone is suing the National Health Service because doctors told him he had three months to live, and three months later the cancer had disappeared. He had given up his job (decorating) and therefore suffered a loss of earnings. A quick word of thanks to the Almighty for sparing his life might seem indicated. But earnings are the better part of life.

Several years back the head of Yorkshire Water encouraged its customers to stop bathing in order to reduce consumption by advancing his own example. He hadn't had a bath or a shower for three months, 'and no one has noticed'. (His wife said that in recent weeks he had spent a lot of time away from home; this would have helped her not to notice.)

Even given a serious crisis—if the whole of Britain sank beneath the waves, there would still be a hose-pipe ban—this is hardly something to boast about. It doesn't seem prudent to inform the public that the commodity you are selling them isn't indispensable, or is necessary only at the rate of half a basinful at infrequent intervals.

It could be—but perish the thought!—that the gentleman, his briefcase stuffed with soap and towels, had been taking surreptitious baths across the border in a neighbouring Water Authority, or enjoyed privileged access to the 103 million gallons that Yorkshire Water is said to lose every day through leaking pipes.

Luckily water doesn't need promoting, for what sort of advertising could the company adopt once the crisis was over?

Truly modest advertising, emanating from Shanghai: 'Our "BEE & FLOWER" SANDALWOOD SOAP, made from selected materials, gives you delightful and lasting fragrance. It not only possesses all the merits a sandalwood scented soap may have, but also does no harm whatever to your skin. Just try it, and you will see our sincere recommendation is rather convincing.'

There was an unassuming London barber, in the eighteenth century, who promoted his services with this inscription over the door:

> Here lives Jemmy Wright,
> Shaves as well as any man in England,
> Almost—not quite.

In his *Notebooks* Geoffrey Madan quotes R. A. Knox: 'The room smelt of not having been smoked in.' That's double-edged enough to please everybody.

THE university having informed successful candidates of their admission on the strength of their HSC results etc., the government suddenly presents a list of names, those who are to be quietly de-admitted, on undivulged security grounds. (How is the unfortunate registrar to go about this? Presumably by pleading clerical error.) In this way, Special Branch will be spared embarrassment.

When yet another crisis flared up in relations with the governing party, some of us teaching in Singapore during the 1960s were disgusted to hear expatriate colleagues declaring, ritually, patronizingly, 'We must remember, this isn't Oxford or Cambridge.' What had Oxford or Cambridge to do with it? In the heat of debate, the temptation was to call for a degree of academic freedom or purity doubtfully to be found in those ancient institutions. One expects much of youthful countries; one hopes for so much.

A little freedom can go a long way. A lot of freedom . . . ?

Encyclopaedias aren't very helpful, preferring to expatiate on free enterprise, free association, free verse, freemasonry; or, more ambitiously, treat the subject fissiparously: 'as interpreted by Hegel', 'as characteristic of liquids at equilibrium'. But that something is difficult or very difficult or even impossible to understand, and that it isn't satisfactorily explained in encyclopaedias, is not held sufficient reason to deny its existence.

One does indeed see that freedom *means* something. It means, for instance, not being confined in prison without just cause. It means being able to believe in some belief; or rather, since believing cannot be easily discerned or tampered with, the ability to practise a belief, given that no injury is caused to others, and to talk about it, preferably to people who choose freely to listen. It means being able to say or do certain things without fear of the gendarme or the executioner; though there are so many certain things to say or do, some of them on the face of it less admirable than others, that to enumerate and enlarge on them would take more time than most of us are free to spare.

In his 'Essay on Freedom' (1928) Robert Walser points out that freedom is something 'which one can never comprehend, sense, consider, and respect variously enough', that 'one should always be bowing inwardly to the pure image of freedom', and 'there must be no pause in one's respect for freedom, a respect which seems to bear a persistent relation to a kind of fear'. He, he confesses, allows himself to be governed by freedom, regulated by it in every conceivable respect, so to speak oppressed by it. 'And with a constancy that amuses me there dwells within me a most outspoken distrust of it, admirable though it be, this freedom, which I almost refrain from mentioning at all.'

And probably one wouldn't mention freedom at all, were it not being mentioned all the time, in books, newspapers, on radio and television, even occasionally in the streets (and, more jocularly or tentatively, at home), which proves that it is an all-important question.

In conclusion, Walser permits himself to say that freedom is difficult and produces difficulties, and a true connoisseur and gourmet of freedom will note and cherish 'all the unfreedoms internal to freedom'. (See *Robert Walser: Selected Stories*, translated by Christopher Middleton.)

This seems decisive, for Walser was Swiss, and would know all about the subject. He spent the last twenty years of his life in mental hospitals. A visitor once asked him if he was writing anything, and this free spirit replied, 'I am not here to write, but to be mad.' The ticklish question persists: 'Free for what?'

Fortune failed to smile on Walser. Kafkaesque *avant la lettre*, he preceded Kafka by five years and was then overtaken by him. He wasn't all that much like Kafka, only just enough to dim recognition of his originality.

Walser was always hard up. He was an awkward customer; he expected to be paid for his labours. In a fascinating book, *The Author and His Publisher*, Siegfried Unseld gives a barely believable (i.e. entirely credible) account of Walser's relations and non-relations with a succession of publishers. One of his books was quite enough for most publishers; then it was somebody else's turn. In one of his stories a publisher tells an author, 'If you don't bring me a successful new novel, then there is little or no point in your coming to me.' But of course. It wasn't too bright of Walser to preface a series of sketches with the claim that the boy who wrote them had died shortly after leaving school. Yet in 1926, responding to a newspaper survey, he answered the question, 'Are there neglected poets among us?' with 'My publishers inform me that they are delighted with me.' He couldn't even give his books away; some actress returned an offering with the words, 'First learn German before you try to write stories.'

One of his more loyal publishers wanted to pay for a trip to India; and another invited him to go to Poland and write a book about the country, or if not Poland, then Turkey. Walser replied, 'Why do writers have to travel as long as they have imagination?' In an essay he asked, 'Does Nature go abroad?'

'Hölderlin deemed it prudent, in other words tactful, to lose his mind when he was thirty-nine,' Walser had written. 'Will the same thing happen to me?' It did, when he reached the age of fifty-one. One must always be wary of what one commits to paper; after almost every sentence: *absit omen*.

The story told at the head of this entry, how did it end? The government professed to lose interest: what did it matter, a few teenage dissidents getting a higher education? And by next year there would be a system in place whereby all candidates for higher education required a 'suitability certificate' (security clearance) before applying for admission. This let the university off the hook. But there was a price; we had lost a brave vice-chancellor during the skirmish.

I STAND by what I have said before, that nothing has *no* effect at all. Had better grant, though, that the effect can be unexpected, even paradoxical. A juvenile fascination with toy soldiers and pictures of naval battles may be succeeded by a detestation of war. In one's childhood there was a quivery grandeur about Empire Day, yet one might grow into something of an anti-imperialist. (And then, in age, revert in some measure to that half-understood mystique.) Granted, effects can be hard to substantiate and gauge. But more often than not common sense is a sound guide. So I stand by what I said, I think.

A recent argument against the formative effects of reading cites Proust's Françoise, who wept copiously over a clinical account of postnatal sufferings in a medical dictionary (not, as the arguer says, a fictional account), yet felt no sympathy whatsoever for the kitchen maid undergoing the same pains—much to the inconvenience of the household and of Françoise in particular.

The prototype (in that sense fictional) patient of the dictionary was implicitly a respectable married woman, suffering a customary and noble consequence of marriage; and thus, by contrast, accentuating the unworthiness of the unmarried, snivelling wretch in the kitchen, who had wantonly 'brought it on herself'.

Which is to suggest that reading, even of medical books, does have some effect, in this case pernicious, by corroding the heartstrings— and conveniently siphoning off what natural sympathies we may possess.

Christina Rossetti made the point neatly. The wagoner whistles 'A froggy would a-wooing go' as his wagon runs over a frog. There's a vast gulf between 'the hypothetic frog' and the mangled 'uninteresting actual frog'.

No doubt we shall feel a little easier in our minds about Bosnia when we hear that Bosnian children, illegal immigrants, are busy picking pockets right here in Wandsworth.

In his book *The Merry Heart*, Robertson Davies refers to one Henry Cockton, a 'thirty-third-rate' comic novelist, whom (he says) none of his readers will ever have read. I certainly hadn't. Later on Davies mentions a book, published in 1848 and very popular in its day, *Valentine Vox*, to do with a ventriloquist and containing an attack on private asylums for the insane. 'Who reads it now?' *Valentine Vox*! I read it at an early age; it was one of the few books in the house (another oddity was *The Well of Loneliness*). The book terrified me; in particular one of the illustrations, of some unfortunate strapped to a bed and having the soles of his feet tickled with a feather. For me it was, as one says, the stuff of nightmares. Now I gather the book had an author, one Henry Cockton.

I see from the London Library copy that Cockton considered his book essentially humorous but with 'a far higher object in view': to expose 'a system teeming with secret cruelties and horrors'. It's a hefty volume; guzzler of words though I was, I couldn't have read it all through (I don't recall the ventriloquist hero), perhaps only the pages surrounding that picture. The illustrations, attributed to a J. Onwhyn, are in the style of the period which to our eyes makes a depiction of a jolly picnic look sinister. The point of tickling the soles of the feet was to transform a perfectly sane man into the semblance of a raving maniac in readiness for the commissioners' tour of inspection.

Since then I've never felt at ease with feathers.

❧

Sydney Smith's lordly quip is famous: 'I never read a book before reviewing it; it prejudices a man so.' In reality the prejudice is often in place beforehand, and insurmountable. Anthony Burgess described the phenomenon some ten years ago: what he was most strongly aware of in reviews was 'a prepared position, a ready-made judgement unqualified by the act of reading'.

In his commonplace book, Jock Murray gave a variant on Smith, overheard at a literary party: 'I like reviewing books because it makes me want to read them.' (That one is paid to do so indicates a simple interpretation of this cryptic saying.) It is true that writing a clever review endears you to the book in question, whether you thought well of it or ill; without it, you wouldn't have written the review that gives you so much satisfaction. A measure of gratitude—say, inserting a few kind or not unkind words at the last moment—is surely in order.

We are told of a 'controversial' film that 'rather than indulging in sex and violence it actively points out the dangers that endless sex and violence has on our imagination'. John Cleland, creator of *Fanny Hill*, put it more touchingly 250 years ago: 'If I have painted Vice in all its gayest colours, if I have decked it with flowers, it has been solely in order to make the worthier, the sublimer sacrifice of it to Virtue.'

'I've actually saved lives.' Is the director of *Crash* wisecracking when he claims that people fasten their seat-belts after seeing the film?

Some critics are far brighter than the authors they review, and locate all sorts of cleverness in what the uninstructed might think is a squalid mess, inventive only in pushing the fashion a few millimetres further. Cf. 'What believer sees a disturbing omission or infelicity? The text, whether of prophet or of poet, expands for whatever we can put into it, and even his bad grammar is sublime.' George Eliot, in a novel grown so famous through its television adaptation that we don't need to bother with such otiose bits of moralizing.

People wonder why Leavis expressed himself so intemperately, for surely things weren't that bad. Maybe they weren't. He was foreseeing things to come.

NATURE notes.
Glow-worms are on the decline. The male insects cannot see the glowing bodies of the females as the countryside is increasingly merged into urban spread. Instead they are lured to barren windows and street lights. And the noise on our roads is drowning the songs the birds sing to attract their mates. Unheard melodies are not always sweeter. Reports say that a large proportion of male birds never reproduce. It used to be thought that birds living near busy roads failed in this respect because they were killed by cars. The theory is now held to apply more closely to humans.

Neurosis or ritual? The cat won't touch his diet food during the day, but eats it with gusto at night, provided that it is served in the bedroom, the right setting for the night. To reach a favourite resting-spot, he jumps on to a high table, from the table to a low chair, from the chair to a chest of drawers, from the chest to the bed. His life would be flat without neuroses or rituals.

We don't see animals as moral beings, but do we really imagine that animals see us as moral beings? Nietzsche, who raised the question, cited the opinion of a talking animal: that humanity was no more than a preconception, a prejudice which animals didn't suffer from.

Ruskin noted that bluets and poppies among the corn teach us that not everything is meant to be eaten.

THE papers are stuffed with recipes and restaurants, the television screen with chefs and *chefs-d'œuvre*, the publishers' lists with exotic cookery books. New editions of famous old dictionaries announce proudly that they include terms from a multitude of international cuisines.

It is a truism that people tend to eat more than usual after a bereavement (e.g. the death of God), to comfort themselves and reaffirm the will to go on living.

An arts programme on Channel 4 tells us that Proust's novel, *Remembrance of Things Past*, could just as well be entitled 'Remembrance of Tastes Past', it being crammed with food and feeding. (Or, depending on which English title you prefer, 'In Search of Lost Mealtime', I suppose.)

It could even better be called 'Remembrance of Flings Past', since —not surprising in a work of its length and breadth—it embraces all sorts of issues and antics dear to the media.

La Cuisine Retrouvée is a compilation by a leading Parisian chef of recipes for all the dishes mentioned in the said novel. In *How Proust Can Change Your Life*—not a book on dieting—Alain de Botton gently chides this sort of thing as artistic idolatry, the combination of 'a literal reverence for objects depicted in art' with 'a neglect of the spirit of art'. In this instance, it could be plain snobbery. 'We're having leg of mutton with Béarnaise sauce, darling, the Duc de Guermantes, such a dear, did you know him? he loved it.'

The madeleine is a boring little cake, hardly improved by dunking it in tea. You need to be Proust for it to have the required effect. Another agent in the involuntary revival of memories was the noise made when a servant knocked a spoon against a plate. This isn't recommended either. If you go round knocking spoons against plates you will soon attract the attention of men in white coats bearing a strait-jacket.

'RILKE was a *jerk*': John Berryman. (NB: 'Many opinions and errors in the Songs are to be referred not to the character Henry, still less to the author': JB.) No, not a jerk, but there is something off-puttingly privileged about Rilke. I don't mean the castles he lodged in, the wealthy, cultivated women he knew—or even his great lyrical gift. One of his most trustworthy admirers speaks of 'the uses of deprivation and adversity' that lie at the core of the *Duino Elegies* and declare themselves elsewhere in his work: the 'gain that is entailed by loss', the elevation of 'strenuous, unrequited love above the comfort and ease of love fulfilled'. Deprivation is best left to the truly deprived to characterize and appraise. Adversity, we know, has its sweet uses; they are often the perquisites of those who don't suffer the particular adversity.

Is it better to have loved and lost than to have loved and won? Or merely more poetic? I have been gently admonished by the admirer quoted above—and less gently by other Germanists—for having, long ago and in a generally appreciative context, described lines in the *Elegies* about Pearls of Suffering and delicate Veils of Endurance as 'really highbrow baby-talk'. Which was ungrateful of me since a thesis largely on Rilke had gained me an Egyptian doctorate. But then again, when I was back in England one of HM's Inspectors asked me by what right I went under the title of Doctor and whether the degree was officially recognized in this country. I had to admit I didn't know. Rilke's revenge.

(After graduating, one of our bright and energetic Singapore students took a job as journalist on the *Straits Times*. It lasted until she wrote a piece beginning 'Better to have loved and caught a dose than never to have loved at all'. The thought provoked the wrath of the government, which was busy enough rooting out social diseases of other kinds, and the paper, not famous for its heroism, banished her to the classified ads. This is a rare case of literary studies causing visible harm.)

Perhaps Rilke is a poet, like Shelley, who means more when you are young. Youth, when the flavour of self-consciousness (a variety of privilege) doesn't offend, indeed is welcome—because you are yourself preoccupied with consciousness of self, however indistinctly, with your own self-realizing self.

Later in life one's self can grow tedious, a burden, like the maligned grasshopper—though maybe no more so than the clamorous selves of others—as it stumbles bruisingly over items of furniture, mental, moral, that surely weren't there before. Being old can be a full-time job; well, we all need to keep busy.

Researchers at the University of Pennsylvania reckon to have found that men's brains (unlike women's) shrink with age, thus causing grumpiness and loss of sense of humour. Don't know about brains shrinking. Everything else, more likely.

'Du musst dein Leben ändern.' (Rilke again.) It's an exhortation you only truly understand and assent to when in effect it is too late. When your life is being forcibly changed for you, beyond your volition or control. No credit there; of no greater value than a deathbed repentance.

But wait, it could be not the brains shrinking, but the skin growing thinner. That increasing need to close the eyes during hospital soaps, the inability to stand the sight of others' pain, real or fictional, or even to hear about it, without a sharp twinge in the nether regions. As for those who kill or abuse children—flog them! cut their balls off! (no such twinge now), or (even though still resolutely against capital punishment) hang the bastards!

Such immoderate agitations can look much like that famous grumpiness and loss of humour.

They tell you of the horny carapace
Of age,
But not of thin skin growing thinner,
As if it's wearing out . . .
To know more isn't to forgive more,
But to fear more, knowing more to fear . . .

❧

WHY we (which 'we' is that?) dislike euphemisms so much—aside from their currency with the sort of people we look down on when no one is looking—is that they call to mind the uneuphemism, afresh, vividly, with more than the usual discomfort. And the uneuphemism takes on the force of a dysphemism.

Some euphemisms don't cut much ice. A senior bank official told me he hadn't been made redundant, it was just a case of 'position elimination'. (He soon found another job, in booming Asia; his new employer, I imagine, didn't think of him as second-hand, but rather as 'pre-owned' by a colleague in the less fortunate West.)

When Leavis was asked if he could suggest someone for a teaching job (it was generally abroad), he would say that so-and-so was at present, he believed, *en disponibilité*. (So-and-so, a former pupil, was 'between engagements', probably in dire need of work.) *En disponibilité*: a truly cheering euphemism; it made one feel like a diplomat waiting to be transferred from one prize post to another.

Disinfection proceeds apace. Back in 1962 Joe Orton and Kenneth Halliwell served six months in prison for stealing or 'wilfully damaging' books belonging to Islington public libraries. Orton had enhanced some of the books with spoof blurbs. In 1995 these 'works' were put on display in the same libraries, the borough librarian explaining that in those far-off days no one was to know etc., but 'over the years we have become proud of Joe Orton as a leading literary figure with local associations'.

We hear that leading figures in sadism and masochism (sometimes softened into 'sadie-maisie') have set up workshops to make the practice as safe as other practices. One of them says, 'Safe S & M is like driving a car. If you don't learn how to do it properly, you can go out there and hurt someone.' What shall we do for audacious self-expression and thrilling aberrancy when everything is certified harmless and unobjectionable?

'On the whole, I think that pornography is loathsome, but for those who are old enough to buy it legally probably not very dangerous. Anyway, I don't need pornography—I've got Wagner.' One can see that Bernard Levin may well have worn himself out in the cause of good causes and the reprobation of bad ones, and he deserves a rest from mucking-out the stables. (He has even put in a word for embattled smokers; back in 1960 he even put in a word for me.) Levin may have been joking; but I wonder if there isn't something a touch graceless about this remark, reminiscent of the feeling among some intellectuals that illiterate, constricted speech is good enough for the plebs, even right and proper. They themselves don't need it, they have the *Oxford English Dictionary*.

It seems there's a National Campaign Against Censorship of the Internet. This must be the only body ready (nay, eager) to use the filthy word 'censorship'. Even those most worried about child pornography (featuring children or for children) seek to avoid it. It's no surprise that one is never quite certain what 'PC' stands for, political correctness or personal computer.

Some writers on the subject dress the word *smut* in quotation marks—implying that only those deficient in sophistication (what, no quotation marks?) and given to hotness under the collar would use it in all its naked naïvety. Or implying that there is no such thing.

'If it offends you, you only have to switch it off', 'If you find it objectionable, you only have to walk out.' About as cogent as saying, If the news distresses you, don't read the papers.

Some censorship is required, even if we call it 'the law'. In 1997 a German couple went on trial, accused of offering on the Internet to kidnap children, torture them in sex 'games', and (a finishing touch) dispose of the bodies of any who died in the process. What form did their defence take—that it was all just a sophisticated joke, no need to get het up?

Again and again people invoke *Areopagitica*, that high-minded discourse, as a sweeping eulogy of freedom of expression and a wholesale condemnation of censorship. They may be loath to buckle down and read what Milton actually wrote, but they should be able to guess at the kind of publications he was defending.

The road of excess leads a few, a very few, to the palace of wisdom. A few who enjoy the benefit of mysterious signposts and inner directives decipherable only by them. For others, the majority, this road leads to the prison, the hospital, the madhouse.

Today—that is, outside entertainment (purgation through pity and fear?)—we are more, and more soberly, concerned with the road of success, which leads to a desirable residence.

'Be good, sweet maid, and let who will be clever.' Must admit to an uncomfortable suspicion that there may be a grain or two of sense in this risible counsel. (Coming, by the way, from the man who reckoned that the Bible was employed as if it were a constable's handbook, or a dose of opium for keeping beasts of burden quiet while overloading them.) In this world, though, to be good it will help to be tolerably clever.

There's a clever saying of Goethe's—clever in the sense of intelligent, knowledgeable, thoughtful—to the effect that if in old age intelligent and thoughtful persons come to set little store by knowledge, it is only because they have asked too much of it and of themselves.

> *Unheroic couplet*
>
> 'I cannot praise a cloistered virtue!'
> But what if it's the only kind in view?

❧

PROSE: words in their best order; poetry: the *best* words in the best order. Coleridge's 'homely definitions' are true of the best poetry but of only workaday prose. Prose deserves the best words quite as much as poetry does.

Poetry often seems to have—what Keats ascribed to a displeasing form of it—a palpable design on us. 'Look at me!' But we shouldn't blame poetry, which can accommodate sublime heights of lowliness, but rather the poet. 'Look at me!' Poetry as myself-expression.

'To paraphrase Clausewitz, prose for Tsvetaeva was nothing but the continuation of poetry by other means (which, in fact, is what prose historically is).' Thus Joseph Brodsky. Czeslaw Milosz: 'Novels and essays serve but will not last./One clear stanza can take more weight/Than a whole wagon of elaborate prose.' But Baudelaire was right: 'Always be a poet, even in prose.'

A note of Paul Valéry's reads, 'Je cherche un mot . . .':

> I look for a word (*says the poet*), a word which should be feminine,
> of two syllables,
> containing P or F,
> ending with a mute letter,
> and a synonym of cracking, breaking up;
> and not learned, not rare.
> Six conditions—at least!

It is suggested that Valéry wrote this while engaged on the poem 'Les Grenades' ('Pomegranates'), and that the answer he found was 'rupture' ('cette lumineuse rupture'). If this is so, the note is an indirect, exemplary definition of poetry. If he wrote the note after finishing the poem, it is an indirect, exemplary definition of practical criticism.

(While in Australia I was told that the epithet 'pommy' or 'pom', as applied to the British, referred to the way the cheeks of new immigrants turned red in the sun and the skin split, looking like a pomegranate. This may have been politeness on someone's part. Lexicographers, with a modest gesture towards 'orig. uncert.', prefer to trace the term to 'Prisoner of His Majesty' or 'Prisoner of Mother England'—in which case, no very dishonourable reference to the first, involuntary colonists.)

In crabby mood Nietzsche observed that the poet conveys his thoughts festively on the carriage of rhythm—'usually because they are incapable of walking'. He also reckoned that the best author would be the one who was ashamed to become a writer.

C. H. Sisson has said, wisely if vainly, that 'One should not write more poetry than one must, and some formula has to be found for passing the time between poems', adding that the conduct of affairs is one way, though probably not the best. While one is seeing the world of affairs, 'what worlds is one not seeing! But at least these avocations prevent one from thinking of oneself as a poet, which for most writers of verse must be very salutary.' (*Art and Action*.)

At my age, to live on the fringes of the literary world is the most one can expect. After all I live on the fringes of life. And maybe, where the literary world is concerned, the fringes are the best place.

And then, caught up in that world, what other worlds would one be missing? (Or might that be a recommendation?)

The very best words in the very best order. A prominent advert in today's paper carries the headline, 'It amazed my friend . . . I said two simple words. And we were escorted to the finest table in the restaurant.'

Ted Nicholas, an American judging by the currency he thinks in, once had a vision of truth: it struck him 'like a bolt of lightening' (*sic*) that all the good fortune he had enjoyed was due to words. Words had brought him in as much as $3,500,000 in a single year, the publication of thirteen best-selling books, a two million dollar home, a Mercedes convertible . . .

And all because of words; words which, refined by him over the years, will work the trick for anyone. For £14.95, plus p. and p., he will send you a copy of his book, *Magic Words That Bring You Riches*, limited edition, 336 pages, revealing the very best words to use in all sorts of circumstances. Among them are seven magic words that will bring you offers of jobs while all about are losing theirs (page 15), magic words that will persuade capable people to work for you for free (page 47), words that will immediately secure you the fascinated attention of any attractive woman/man you happen to meet (page 23), words that will enable you (a bit of an anticlimax, this) to rent a Mercedes for the price of a Ford (page 25). And that's just for starters.

But what about the two simple words that will get you and your lady/gentleman friend the most desirable table in any restaurant in the world, remote from draughty doors, kitchen smells and WCs? Mr Nicholas isn't telling, not until you buy his book and look up page 9. Could they be—uttered while you hold out a fistful of dollars—'For you'?

If for any reason you are not delighted with the book, you may return it, undamaged, for a prompt and courteous refund of your money. Much to gain, nothing to lose; it's Pascal's wager yet again. Mr Nicholas isn't likely to make a fortune out of his book. (But he's made his fortune already.)

Heine wasn't far wrong when he said, 'The world is the signature of the word.' Further evidence of this fateful confusion comes more recently from Greg Delanty, in his youth a compositor: 'Every time I read the word *world* I wonder/is it a typo and should I delete the *l*' ('The Composing Room').

CHARITIES are hell-bent on killing charity. Subscribe to one of them, and a hundred others pounce on your name and never let go. There follow phone calls seeking to enlist you in some local campaign, trotting from door to door with a collecting box or erecting a marquee in a nearby field. You plead that you are advanced in years and rather lame, and as it happens so is your wife. 'Will you be able to help us in a couple of months?' All you know is that in a couple of months you'll be that much older. You are forced to the unhappy conclusion that charity had better begin at home and stay there.

Donkey's years ago, when *The Spectator* printed a poem of mine about an unloved child, I asked the magazine to send the fee to the NSPCC as a donation. Ever since, I have received letters from the charity, conscientiously forwarded by the magazine, detailing ways in which 'your company and employees' can support the organization. I have no company or employees, not a single share in *The Spectator*, and have explained to the NSPCC (with whom I have a modest covenant *in propria persona*) how this misconception arose. To no avail. I still get brochures urging me to enter into corporate partnership and listing the benefits accruing, such as 'image enhancement' and 'publicity opportunities'. Charity begins at head office.

Once a computer has logged you and assigned you to some role, however unreal, you are trapped. Even death will offer no escape from its claws.

'There are many myths and misunderstandings about wills and legacies.' After which stirring overture, this pre-eminently deserving charity now offers me a free guide, 'in plain English, without legal jargon', on how to make or change a will, and include 'a simple addition, called a Codicil', whereby a legacy (or 'the residue of your estate') is left to the charity. They're getting money from me while I'm alive; now they want money when I'm dead. That's *big* business for you.

Everything has a price. Prices fascinate us. We like to know what other people are getting for our money. Clever charities tell us, often with the aid of pictures, what a donation of (tick the box) £5, £17.50, £35, £110 etc. will provide. M.U.A.C. (Measurement of Upper Arm Circumference) tapes, identifying the degree of malnourishment in children, cost 17p each, and scales £34, while 25p will buy a plastic beaker, £41 a large metal cooking pot, and £3 (feeding the malnourished is a 24-hour operation) a hurricane lamp.

Prices enforce a sense of immediate reality—more compelling than those pictures of emaciated children, from which (one skeleton is much like another) we avert our eyes.

If you are to go on giving money you will need to keep your strength up. One appeal offers a 'tantalizing' recipe devised by a celebrity chef, for chicken with squash, pineapple, root ginger, and a special chilli sauce. The latter, imported from Swaziland, is marketed by the charity in question.

Personalized appeals can be irritating, particularly those which repeat your name, Mr X, at regular intervals to show just how personal they are. (The one advising me, 'Whatever you do, don't get old' was a bit near the knuckle, I felt.) Even so, it's easier to throw away those addressed to 'the Occupier'. He or she is probably some poor old nameless pensioner.

A device used by one charity concerned with feeding African children—a version of casting breadcrumbs upon the waters—is to send you two penny coins, with the request that you, the X family, return them along with anything else you can possibly afford, since everything costs so many pounds plus 2p. The sight of two pathetic brown pennies lying on your breakfast table pricks the conscience, the first time round. Subsequently a horrid suspicion creeps in that you are being blackmailed. 'God bless you!' the letter ends. There's an implied threat there.

And those sad, disastrous pennies? There's bound to be some collecting box you can surreptitiously drop them in.

Not long ago I sent a small cheque to a charity engaged in providing for starving children in Africa; most likely the one mentioned above. The same evening the doorbell rang, and there stood a real live African. He explained haltingly that he worked for an organization that sent books and computers to Africa. It's true, man doesn't live by bread alone. I didn't have any computers to dispose of, I told him, but I could certainly give him books. 'Books?' he said incredulously. 'Well, you want books, didn't you say?' 'No, I want donations,' he explained patiently. 'Not books, *money*.'

Stay at home, and the whole unhappy world will beat a path to your door.

The kindness of strangers. A sorrowful yet (another fallen word?) uplifting letter of thanks in the local paper. A couple were in a Wandsworth restaurant when the wife was taken ill. 'She did not make it and as a result made somewhat of a mess,' the husband writes. The staff cleaned up promptly, cheerfully, without a hint of reproach. 'I indicated that my wife had cancer and this was most likely to be our last dinner out together.' When his wife returned, the man asked for the bill, and wasn't allowed to pay. He tried to leave a tip, but they wouldn't accept it.

The wife died three weeks later.

※

IN its promotional literature (must find a substitute for that last word) *Granta* quotes an encomium, 'the most impressive literary magazine of its time', and continues hastily, 'the word "literary" may be troubling you'. Actually it wasn't. 'It also troubles us,' the editor confides. I'm sorry to hear that.

In a publisher's catalogue a new work of fiction is described as 'at once literate and literary'. Qualities, we assume, which are generally considered incompatible.

Signs of the times. The Folio Society, long acclaimed for its handsome editions of the classics and other superior items, heads an advertisement in the press: 'Our books aren't just good looking. They're also good in bed', and closes with the injunction 'So don't just lie back and think of England. Join the Folio Society.' Some promotional person will be pleased with him/herself for so adroitly catching the Zeitgeist as it lurches from bed to worse.

A serious and appreciative review of a production of Britten's *The Turn of the Screw* is headlined 'The best Screw of my whole life', while another paper carries an advert for BBC Radio 4's 'Book at Bedtime': 'LISTEN TO OTHER PEOPLE MAKE LOVE IN YOUR BED'. Not especially appealing, I would have thought.

A 'quality' paperback club introduces a variation: 'QPD readers do it in the bath!' Cf. a Mercury advert: 'Talk Dirty with a Friend in Bath'. And Waterstone's proclaim: 'There is one thing the British like to do with the bedroom light on'. And now, as two passions meet, the blurb for a book entitled *Better Than Sex Cookbook* promises 'Food That Makes Love To Your Tastebuds'.

Sex sells books. What do books sell?

(It seems unwise of Waterstone's to inscribe their give-away bookmarks with this Shakespearian tag: 'A snapper up of unconsidered trifles'; and the same could be said, in another line of business, of the self-styled Impact School of Motoring. A leading American manufacturer put their foot in it when they named a new style of women's shoe 'Incubus'. It sounded good. Lawyers checked for any possible violation of trademark, and found it original. But nobody thought to consult a dictionary for any possible prior meaning.)

I gather from Beryl Bainbridge, invited by her German publisher to this year's Frankfurt Book Fair, that the city's ladies of the night take their holidays during the Fair, because there are now so many women in publishing. I think I see what is meant.

AN unquiet presence. 'What follows then, under the rubric of the death of the author, is at one and the same time a statement of the return of the author . . . the concept of the author is never more alive than when pronounced dead.' Thus Seán Burke in *The Death and Return of the Author*. Well—one supposes—said. Some literary theorists do have a way with words; it seems a pity they waste themselves on literary theory. Derrida wanted to write literature, while philosophy ('What is Literature?') was merely meant to be a detour—one from which so far he hasn't extricated himself.

The death of God . . . the death of the author. The latter phenomenon 'might be said to fulfil much the same function in our day' as did the former in the late nineteenth century. A little mortifying from God's point of view, rather like being kicked when one is down. But Seán Burke ties the thought up neatly: 'The author has thus become the object of a residual antitheology, as though the Satan of *Paradise Lost* had suddenly redirected his rebellion against the unsuspecting figure of Milton himself.' Hard on Milton, who did his best to avoid using the term 'author' of himself, preferring to reserve it for the (then living) 'Author of all being', and waiving his own copyright: 'Sing, Heav'nly Muse'.

As an idea the death of the author generates a singularly limited interest. Writers on the topic say much the same thing over and over—varying the phraseology (if only by speaking in tongues known and unknown), switching references, shifting the angle slightly—to a degree that no 'author' could get away with. It's rather like scanning a series of obituaries of the same person: one comes to think that the deceased must have had a narrow, repetitious life, even cracking the same jokes, good though they may have been, to every potential obituarist within hearing.

We have to grant that the proper way to tackle the theorists—not by swearing, jeering, grinding the teeth—lies in using their language, meeting them on their ground, getting inside them. Except that, once inside, you will never get out, your ingenuities will be indistinguishable from theirs, your confutations sound like confirmations. For within literary theory only literary theory is of any significance, and only within literary theory is literary theory of any significance.

Burke ends his book in the mode which has lingered from his title onwards: a circular motion, giving with one hand and taking away with the other. 'Indeed a concerted programme of authorial reinscription may well be inconceivable under the banner of literary theory; it could even be that since theory became possible with the exclusion of the author, the author signals the impossibility of theory.' Fair enough, you would say. However, 'This is a conclusion to be resisted, and one that can only be resisted by theorists themselves . . .' We are bound to ask who else would want to resist it.

Burke's closing sentence partakes of poetry. The question of the author, a question questioning theory and its reach and adequacy, poses itself 'in the manner of an interminable haunting, as that unquiet presence which theory can neither explain nor exorcize'. Which is about as ecumenical as we can hope to get amid a host of banners bearing strange devices.

Being queasy by-products of capitalist ideology, and naturally concerned for readers and the upkeep of their numbers, authors may find it marginally easier to reconcile themselves in the light of Roland Barthes's pronouncement: 'The birth of the reader must be at the cost of the death of the Author.'

In an essay, 'Standing up for Literature', Roger Shattuck deplores the separation of literature and teaching, the invasion of the humanities by 'politics' (in the broad sense of the term), and the handing over of literature to preconception, programme, or (that tricky word, for literature *is* relevant) 'relevance'. During one of his classes at Boston University, a young woman chose for comment Emily Dickinson's light-hearted poem, 'A Bird came down the Walk'. It was, she maintained, 'really' about a lesbian sexual encounter, as witness the lines, 'And then he drank a Dew/From a convenient Grass'. (Never mind that the bird happened to be male: it's just cross-dressing.) The young woman had been encouraged in this interpretation by some other literature course she had followed. And, she added, there were several references to the clitoris in the poem.

I can't quite see where, except conceivably (inconceivably) in 'He bit an Angleworm in halves/And ate the fellow, raw', and 'he unrolled his feathers/And rowed him softer home'. Softer, mark you, 'Than Oars divide the Ocean,/Too silver for a seam—/Or Butterflies, off Banks of Noon/Leap, plashless as they swim'. Make what you will of that.

Serious-minded seekers after relevance might find the issue of ecology/traffic menace more urgently present. After drinking the dew, the poor hard-pressed creature, stirring his velvet head 'like one in danger', 'hopped sidewise to the Wall/To let a Beetle pass'.

'As innocent as gay . . . unfortunately as gay as innocent' (*Guy Mannering*). Translating a letter of Proust's, one sees that the correct, literal rendering is 'two gay men, full of love of life'. Obviously that won't do. So, 'merry men'? No, Robin Hood's . . . God rest you merry . . . Doubtless one will find a way round it, but resentfully, sourly, one's 'homophobia' stirring.

'The Master said: "The poem *The Ospreys* is gay without lasciviousness and sad without bitterness."' 'Needless to say . . . ,' Simon Leys remarks in his translation of Confucius, but goes on notwithstanding to say so, in an acerbic footnote concerning the 'hijacking' of words. For the Master also said: 'In the matter of language, a gentleman leaves nothing to chance.'

('Do we really need another lament on the misuse of words like "gay"?' someone asks wearily. 'The lexicological tide has swept by, and there is nothing anybody can do about it.' It was observed of that perfect English gentleman, Sir Charles Grandison, that he never frighted gay company with grave deliberations; but some lost causes warrant a continued lament.)

The second line of Lawrence Durrell's *Antrobus Complete* (1985) ends with the word 'portentious'. Possibly a confusion with the spelling of 'pretentious', though not, the context makes plain, with its meaning. 'Portentous' just doesn't sound right, it needs a 'sh' somewhere, as in 'bumptious', 'factitious', 'contentious'; it derives from the Latin, 'to stretch out', and it could do with stretching out or slurring a bit. It's a word one always thinks twice about, uncertain of quite what it portends.

Ah, the decay of language! A supermarket sells 'cod pieces' at its fish counter.

❧

'THE more a man cultivates the arts, the less he fornicates. Only the brute really gets it up. Fornication is the lyricism of the people.' Thus Baudelaire, some time ago. Further back, Montaigne speculates that a mule-driver makes a more vigorous lover than a gentleman, because the gentleman has emotions, and emotions undermine the body's strength.

Authors of fiction soaked in sweaty sex, confidently ingenious, hopefully startling, should take to heart (no doubt they have hearts in civilian life) an Indian verse dating from the second century:

> Bookish lovemaking
>   is soon repetitive:
> It's the artless customer
>   with his own style
> wins my heart.
>
>   (translated by Arvind Krishna Mehrotra)

We are frequently told, ah but these sex scenes are *funny*, i.e. mature readers laugh, or rather they smile, they don't get hot under the collar or elsewhere. Humour's a tricky business, but in this field I can't think of many things funnier than another verse from the same source:

> Always wanting me
> to come on top
> and complaining
> we're childless,
> as if you could fill
> an inverted waterjug.

XY's new novel comes in two versions, one for the UK, the other for the USA. In the latter the heroine has a good—sorry, has highly enjoyable sex on page 4, in the former not until page 12. This has been held to show that the British are more subtle than the Americans, more inclined to the sophisticated and oblique, willing to wait for their pleasures. Such strange occasions we find for self-congratulation.

Reading Jostein Gaarder's *Sophie's World*, one keeps hoping Sophie isn't going to be raped or murdered. The philosophy lessons are nicely done, illuminated with homely instances; one can follow them with fair ease. (Some of the time.) But teachers can't always be trusted with pupils, not even teachers of philosophy. ('Philosophy is not a harmless party game.') One keeps hoping.

Does this mean one is a sentimental slob, or a trivial-minded reader shamefacedly anticipating—what is still more easily understood—rape or murder? The suspicion lingers that, despite appearances, one is embarked on yet another contemporary novel.

Book finished. (Not without effort.) Well done, Mr Gaarder, done without murder or rape. You have failed to write a contemporary novel. What could be more honourable? And you have written the unlikeliest best seller ever.

'Realist', 'realism': arrogant terms in literary discourse, so sure of themselves, pretending to 'reality', the truth, the whole truth, and hence unassailable, undeniable. Until someone does deny them.

Lots of (for want of a better word) sex in Salman Rushdie's novels; but magical-realist rather than 'realistic'. And therefore more realistic. If by that word you mean an approach to the real thing.

Artfulness—the converse of sweatiness—does help. There's something inspiriting in Chekhov's account of a Japanese prostitute in action, so skilled that 'you feel you are not having intercourse so much as taking part in a top-level equitation class'.

But it's a poem from the thirteenth-century *Carmina Burana* that should have the last word, or so you might think:

> Pictured on a canvas
> Roses bear false witness,
> For those who paint the bloom
> Deny its true perfume.

Ah, but roses and perfumes: that's going it a bit! Beware of excitement. Bear in mind the cautionary tale of Gauguin, getting worked up over the charms of Tahiti. Behind excitement there lurks something offensive to our modern susceptibilities, something barely mentionable. 'Troubling' is the word used by those who aren't altogether convinced but prefer not to stick their necks out. To desire a woman is to make women *disponible*! (Another good word gone west.)

> 'Safe sex'! Can this be
> What we've all been waiting for—
> Or just a wet dream?

IRONY, I see, is taking another beating. It's merely defensive, self-protective, evasive, it's a coward's camouflage, you ought to come out from behind it and face up to—up to whatever it is. True, a regiment of ironizing paratroopers wouldn't win a war. But that's war, while what we're talking about is—war, too. Figuratively speaking. And what's the alternative strategy in this figurative war? Tirade. At least the deployment of irony doesn't end in making you indistinguishable from your opponents. (Though it may lose a few friends.) It can even raise a subversive laugh.

Irony as feel-good factor. (God knows, one feels bad much of the time.) Goethe noted that, though they couldn't act, the powerless or overpowered might still express their views in speech. (Primitive times, those.) He quoted Mazarin who, on being shown some satirical songs on a new tax, said: 'Let them sing, as long as they pay.' He didn't grudge them their consolatory ironies.

An addition to that disputed category of situational irony: billboards outside the Yvonne Arnaud Theatre in Guildford announcing forthcoming productions of Shakespeare and Oscar Wilde—'MACBETH, AN IDEAL HUSBAND'.

Poetry itself—a way of preventing something or other you can't defeat from getting the better of you. 'Bring your drugs, Art of Poetry—they do relieve the pain at least for a while' (a poet). Unheroic, it's true. 'Unhappy the land that has no heroes!' 'No, unhappy the land that needs heroes' (another poet). Men's foreheads will go on bleeding without the help of truncheons or rifle butts (a third poet).

If one took *Faust* seriously—it's always been considered a deeply serious work, of course, but that's not the same thing—one might well boggle at the Lord's cavalier rationalization of Mephistopheles. Men are only too prone to lapse into lethargy, so he is to be a proactive companion to them, one who will stir them up in his devilishly creative way. Why, Mephistopheles is practically one of us, the Lord is saying, part of the Grand Design! We must assume that the Lord is not indulging in evasive irony. He is simply more honest, or (in his jocular manner) more persuasive, than most of those mortals who have tackled the theodicean problem: evil is permitted because without it we should fall asleep.

Mephistopheles—the 'unwitting stimulus to good', as the scholars have it—makes friends with Faust and keeps him up to scratch. As a result, it's not a case of Gretchen's forehead bleeding where no wounds were: her head is chopped off by the executioner. And Mephistopheles (where did he get that fancy name?) is only a *minor* devil, a 'rogue' according to the Lord, though David Luke gives reasons for translating the epithet 'Schalk' as 'ironic scold' or 'ironist'. Give a poodle a bad name and he'll hang you.

Naturally the Lord isn't altogether wrong about Mephistopheles, as things turn out. After a few casualties en route, and a touch of verbalistic sharp practice, Faust is saved from damnation and consigned to the tutelage of Gretchen, by now quite at home in her new surroundings.

Faust had to be seen to be saved, but the last grand-operatic spectacular on the outskirts of heaven looks rather like a stopgap on the part of the 81-year-old author. Goethe wasn't given to *finishing*, he couldn't let go of his major works. Had he lived even longer, he might have gone back and saved Gretchen from the sword. His nature, as he said, was conciliatory, and one of his most resonant outbursts was directed at those who considered him a heathen: 'After all, I had Gretchen executed . . . Isn't that Christian enough for these people?' As if he regretted doing it.

Irony, these people are telling me, is out. Look at this television commercial. It seems to be for package holidays, or an exotic fruit drink. A hint of irony, they say, would ruin it. They show me another commercial, probably for breakfast food; the colours are blinding. Same thing. And the same with comedy: they show a clip, laced with laughter. The slightest trace of irony would kill it dead. Because, they say firmly, irony is closely related to death. Death.

With that word still echoing, the dull dream ends. I wake up thirsting for the exciting ironies I sense hovering nearby, and even for death, that being the price. There are worse ways to start the day.

※

IN August 1995 an examiner describes the enlivening oddities he has come across in pupils' literature scripts. One is the King Charles's head syndrome. Thus, 'I want to stop discussing *The Mayor of Casterbridge* for a moment in order to talk about Jesus', or a sudden shift from Willis Hall's play, *The Long and the Short and the Tall*, into 'the greater problem of nuclear disarmament and what the West needs to do about it'.

Apposite remarks occurring in term papers by students of modern history at Canadian universities:

'Germany was morbidly overexcited and unbalanced. Berlin became the decadent capital, where all forms of sexual deprivations were practised. A huge anti-semantic movement arose. Attractive slogans like "Death to all Jews" were used by governmental groups.'

'War screeched to an end when a nukuleer explosion was dropped on Heroshima.'

'A whole generation had been wiped out in two world wars, and their forlorne families were left to pick up the peaces.'

'At war people get killed, and then they aren't people any more, but friends.'

In the simpler mode of *1066 and All That*, these specimens from American classrooms were reported some years earlier by a teacher in Concord, New Hampshire:

'The inhabitants of ancient Egypt were Mummies. They travelled by Camelot.'

'The Greeks invented three kinds of column—Corinthian, Doric, and Ironic. They also had myths. A myth is a female moth.'
'The government of England was a limited mockery.'
'Sir Francis Drake circumcised the world with a 100-foot clipper.'
'When Elizabeth exposed herself before her troops, they all shouted "Hurrah". Then her navy went out and defeated the Spanish armadillo.'

The curious, heart-warming pleasure these howlers generate in us has nothing to do with feelings of superiority. Rather, they make a change from the deadly knowingness that prevails in other quarters. And sometimes these comical errors awaken sorrowful truths: '. . . left to pick up the peaces', '. . . they aren't people any more, but friends'.

My favourites are those I met at first hand. In Egypt (by an indigenous confusion between 'b' and 'p'): '. . . this Age of Atomic Pomp'; in Thailand (the sort of terse encapsulation enjoined by a taxing climate): 'Milton wrote this book [*Paradise Lost*] for telling men how the was happened and why people must.' Anti-semantic perhaps, but poignantly accurate.

❧

AM reading a new young poet, much touted. Presumably postmodern. (A term that's supposed to explain everything.) At any rate, packed with detail, images and quirks, a butterfly curiosity, a weird disembodied liveliness. No sneering, no air of superiority; hardly any air at all. No suspicion (it doesn't need saying) of moral implication or animus. The interest is on the surface; there are no roots, no relations. Out of quite a lot, nothing much comes. Farewell (and some will say good riddance) to revelation. After the initial attraction and the expectation aroused, what's left is a sense of muzziness, a faint queasiness. (Tell me what I am to feel, give me just a hint!) Some literature is aspiring towards the condition of some music.

'Mrs Robson's parrots would not allow any reading aloud in their presence unless their own names were frequently introduced. If they heard these interspersed among the reading they would be quiet, for they believed it was all about themselves; they did not understand it, but no matter what it was, it must be all right if it was about them.'

Mr Peter Scupham, a scholar, sends me this passage from Samuel Butler's *Notebooks*, justly emending 'parrots', patently a misprint, to 'poets'. We may assume that Mrs Robson was the mistress of a salon, possibly one of those that used to forgather in North London drawing-rooms and Soho hostelries. Her worthy successors are active in poetry coteries and societies. 'We have our *own* little Arts Council here,' one of them once told me. Another confided, '*My* poets eat out of my hand. I never give them anything to drink before a performance.'

There are also those poets who are inured to not hearing their names introduced, and content that it should be so. They know that 'Who's a pretty boy, then?' is never meant for them.

(Incidentally, it was Butler who recorded an oral misprint in a child's prayer: 'Forgive us our christmasses as we forgive them that christmas against us.')

Talks, poetry readings etc.—never make jokes, never make your listeners laugh. At the time they may chortle uproariously, with every sign of enjoyment, if only because of the solemnity and portentousness they are accustomed to. But later, 'funny, yes, but . . .', as if *post coitum*; and up goes their opinion of the solemn portentousness: it may have been a trifle heavy-going, even largely inaudible, but it was solid, serious-minded stuff.

As Rochester perceived,

> For wits are treated just like common whores,
> First they're enjoyed, and then kicked out of doors.

Yet 'Parnassus has many mansions' (Auden). Some of them poky, poorly furnished, frequented by seedy, impudent and ill-conditioned characters. It takes all sorts. There's an unrhymed line, in a poem by Mary Fullerton (Australian, born in 1868), which (through a species of pun!) effortlessly conjures up its tacit rhyme: 'And in God's house are many scansions.'

Many mansions, many scansions . . . But I can't abide those poets who call their products 'The' when it ought to be 'A': 'The Gaza Triptych', 'The Bosnia Elegy', 'The London Sequence'. As if they were writing definitively, pronouncing the ultimate word. As if literature—let alone life—had no past and no future. The great Landlord is not to be mocked.

A *Financial Times* review of a new book by a famously clever poet begins, 'I once read, or heard it remarked, that "There's a lot of cleverness in the world, but not enough."' Sounds much like the closing line of a poem, c.1960, unmemorably entitled 'In Memoriam', to do with Japan and a friend there, a teacher, dying of cancer. There's fame for you! My name is Anon.

How shall you sing the Lord's song in a strange land? But where else would you sing? At home? Home is where you hang up your harp; home is sweet in your absence, in the absence of your singing. There are other definitions of home: it's a manifold, equivocal, shifting concept; you experience it, wherever you experience it, fitfully; home today is away tomorrow, away today is home tomorrow, that's how you tell the one from the other.

    Songs are at home in strange places. That's where they are needed, at least by the singer. Where shall you sing the Lord's song, or any other song? By the waters of Babylon, for instance, whether or not they ask you to.

'CRITICS who say that the potential of the Internet is over-hyped are either ignorant or arrogant (or both).' The potential for good is what's meant. I've been reading earnest articles on information technology, all of them unstintingly enthusiastic. One trivial disadvantage is casually envisaged: the rich are likely to get richer, the poor poorer, just as the clever will grow cleverer, the stupid stupider, but that's an old story, it happens all the time irrespective.

One would feel more inclined to trust the champions of the new technology if they spared a few moments from predicting the glorious benefits in store to look at the possible ill effects. 'We presume to welcome Prometheus while overlooking Pandora' (Roger Shattuck). I can't say what the ill effects may be, and prefer to keep my imagination on a tight rein. (Never forget that medieval axiom: 'A powerful imagination generates the event.') Let's say, alienation from fellow humans (also its seeming opposite, an unhealthy coalescence), and from our actual (as opposed to virtual) environment; complexities rendered down into simplicities, and simplicities blown up into complexities; injury caused by undirected (or, come to that, directed) surfing; insult to the brain arising from info overload (or drowning in it; Arthur C. Clarke comments that getting information from the World Wide Net is like trying to fill a glass of water from Niagara Falls); the end of privacy; the subverting of marriage and the nuclear family, and the transformation of children into creatures resembling John Wyndham's Midwich Cuckoos; a boom in criminal opportunity; local malice and large conflicts (cyberspace propaganda wars have broken out between Palestinian and Israeli www sites) . . . As ever, it's not the technology that one fears; it's man whom, and for whom, one fears.

A recent report states that X-rated content—also known as 'inappropriate material'—is the biggest money earner on the Net, and one of its champions claims that the Internet will change human sexuality by offering information and education and 'the chance of a first step for the timid', besides providing 'a means of contacting others with similar sexual preferences'.

This mode of access and communication does have a lot to be said for it. There's no need to get out of bed for it; wherever you may be, it's brought to you promptly—in this much like pizza, or like death as perceived by Kingsley Amis.

A new-style agony aunt is much in demand.

'Junk e-mail pours in daily with offers of Russian brides, weight loss etc. It's driving me crazy. What can I do?'

'My computer has a t-t-terrible s-s-stutter . . .'

'My mouse pointer keeps jumping around on the screen . . .'

'My fax modem has stopped answering the phone. What shall I do?'

'What is a "cookie"? I am told that I have been sent them when I open my Internet connection. Should I accept them? Are they good or bad?'

But maybe we can domesticate the technology by subtle and humane recourse to the pathetic fallacy. A 'virtual temple' has been set up on the Internet, presided over by the head priest of a Zen Buddhist temple in Kyoto, in which memorial services can be held for defunct software—extinct computer games, dead bits and bytes of information, long departed Russian brides and putrefied cookies, expired messages and lifeless e-mailed love letters (see the MLA paper on the sentimental culture of the Internet), and so forth. The rationale inspiring this initiative, as disclosed by the *Far Eastern Economic Review*, has it that a computer program is a structure animated for a certain period of time by a succession of tiny electric impulses—and so is a human being.

That should put it in its place.

Giving your books to people is a way of losing friends. Goethe observed that should someone come across a book by accident or recommendation he may read it, he may even buy it, but if the author, a friend, presents the book, it will seem that he means to demonstrate his intellectual predominance. Worth bearing in mind, no matter how amiable your intention. Such behaviour partakes of that new crime, stalking, and the proffering of unwelcome flowers or boxes of chocolates.

The young man at the bank where I have kept a modest account for the past sixty years professes his eagerness to help me in any way possible, I being an old and valued customer. I try to think of a way. Over the phone he asks if I am finding something to do, and answers himself, 'Gardening, I suppose?' He can't believe I am capable of stringing words together. I send him a (remaindered) book of mine, and never hear from him again. I must have hurt his feelings. Should have left it at gardening.

'Finding something to do, eh?' When the city of Corinth was threatened with assault, all its inhabitants rushed to defend it: digging ditches, shoring up the walls, sharpening weapons, gathering an arsenal of stones. Seeing this, Diogenes took to rolling his barrel energetically back and forth through the streets. When asked why he was behaving thus, he replied that he just wanted to be busy like everyone else, he didn't intend to be the only idler in the city.

This is an emblem of age, which wants to be doing things, no matter how trifling they are. Kierkegaard's remark that Diogenes couldn't conceivably be hailed as a benefactor of Corinth, let alone its saviour, is beside the point.

Some institutions still provide that heart-warming service, the personal touch. Over the phone: 'Yes, Mr X, how can I help you ... It is my pleasure, Mr X', and so on. Alas, we now learn from a television documentary that these civilities are flashed up on the employee's computer, with such injunctions as 'REPEAT CUSTOMER'S NAME'. Perhaps it was his computer that prompted the young man at the bank into enquiring how I passed my declining years: 'SHOW INTEREST'.

'No customer contact,' declares a young woman in the same documentary as she caresses her computer. 'I prefer it that way.' (Did someone once press a book on her?) The programme ends with a company director, heavily jowled and lugubrious of aspect, speaking of the day, not far off, when the young man, the young woman, won't be needed either, since whole transactions will be carried out by self-regulating computers. Asked if he doesn't feel some unease at this abrogation of humanity, he mumbles, 'I have nothing against technology.' As a human, he looks pretty close to the end of his shelf-life.

❧

'IN the sweat of thy face shalt thou eat bread, till thou return unto the ground.' It was not as a punishment that work followed the Fall. It came as a palliative.

Or, as Alain viewed the process of growing up: 'I was nourished by rivers of milk; but that could not last. They drove me out of that paradise because I wanted to be driven out; and I work out this punishment, which is my own richness.'

'The more one works, the better one works, and the more one wants to work . . . One can forget time only by making use of it.' Thus Baudelaire. And Seamus Heaney ('An Artist'): '. . . working as the only thing that worked'.

There is a moment in each day, Blake said, that Satan cannot find, nor can his watch-fiends. But the industrious find this moment and multiply it, and when once it is found it can renovate every moment of the day.

In one of those rubbishy supplements that the quality papers think fit to churn out at the weekends, a writer—young, judging by the photograph—confides that there is something in her which always wants to do something other than writing. Being alone all day is 'psychologically damaging', as she realizes when she goes to the shops and is scared to find she has to talk to people. Moreover, 'when you sit around all day, you feel your bum spreading'.

Georges Simenon once said that writing is not a profession but a vocation of unhappiness. Even so, he published over 400 books.

In the old days the aged were disposed of by leaving them to starve to death. These days they are starved of work, to something of the same effect. The trend has speeded up, embracing the middle-aged, and ('till thou return unto the ground'?) heading for the young. 'Done because we are too menny,' the boy explained before he hanged himself.

He wants to make the job last. Last him out. Who knows when another will come along? Clearly modern technology—time-saving!—is to be avoided, though he allows himself a typewriter, antique, slow-moving and prone to break down. Even Tipp-Ex is suspect: do the whole page again! Moreover—there is no end to the man's cunning, in another profession he could have made millions—he uses an old ribbon, not quite the right size, so the ascenders and serifs have to be inked in. The job is going to last. (Will he?)

EARLY in Italo Calvino's *If on a winter's night a traveller* there is a scene in a bookshop, obviously one of those very big ones. You come upon stout barricades of Books You Haven't Read, acres and acres of Books You Needn't Read, Books Made for Purposes Other Than Reading, Books Read Even Before You Open Them Since They Belong To The Category Of Books Read Before Being Written, Books That If You Had More Than One Life You Would Certainly Read, Books Too Expensive Now So You'll Wait Till They're Remaindered, Books That Everybody's Read So It's As If You Had Read Them Too, and so on and on.

At last you find the book you wanted, which happens to be *If on a winter's night a traveller* by Italo Calvino. You pick up a copy and carry it to the cashier. 'You cast another bewildered look at the books around you (or, rather: it was the books that looked at you, with the bewildered gaze of dogs who, from their cages in the city pound, see a former companion go off on the leash of his master, come to rescue him), and out you went.'

All perfectly authentic, except for the last bit. Those massed books don't gaze at you in bewilderment; they glare at you haughtily, contemptuously: '*You* couldn't have written us, we're far too grand for *you*, within the hour all of us will have gone . . . don't bother to count your pitiful coins.'

Theodor Adorno's experience on visiting a book fair was rather different. He realized that books no longer looked like books. They were ashamed of still being books, they did their best not to look like anachronisms. Dignity had disappeared—maybe driven out by their jackets—and now 'the book sidles up to the reader; it no longer presents itself as existing in itself but rather as existing for something else, and for this very reason the reader feels cheated of what is best in it'.

'The life of the book is not coterminous with the person who imagines it to be at his command,' Adorno says in the same piece, 'Bibliographical Musings'. 'What gets lost in a book that is loaned out and what settles into a book that is sheltered are drastic proof of that.' (What gets lost in a book that is loaned out is often the book.) Some time ago I sent my dilapidated copy of Eliot's *Collected Poems 1909–1935*, a school prize, to Changi Prison to be rebound. And so it was, indestructibly, though the edges of the pages had been trimmed as if by a scalpel (presumably under careful supervision) and the marginal scribblings accumulated over many years were lost. I no longer understand *The Waste Land*.

Can't resist cribbing a story from Anthony Powell's journals, about the bookshop assistant asked if they had a copy of *Prometheus Unbound*: 'No, but I'm almost sure I've seen a bound copy on the shelves.'

> And I had seen on the price-tag that it cost £23.00:
> Small wonder that the custom of snipping off the price
> As an exercise in social deportment has simply died out;
> Indeed a book today is almost worth buying for its price,
> Its price frequently being more remarkable than its contents.

As the convent goes up in flames, it strikes a sprightly nun that her brother-in-law's niece isn't going to get her copy of Conor Cruise O'Brien back. And after it costing somebody so much! (Paul Durcan's 'Six Nuns Die in Convent Inferno'.)

'Books have the same enemies as men: fire, damp, animals, time; and their own contents': Valéry.

Habent sua fata libelli. The British Council—it cannot please all the people all the time, but quite easily displeases many of them much of the time—has recently been under fire for closing down some of its overseas libraries.

After I left Bangkok in 1959 under a cloud of ambiguities, the wife of the Council's Representative went through the library removing my books. There must have been six of them; were they shredded, I wonder, or consumed on a bonfire, as happened to the country's opium pipes at about the same time.

In the wake of the above, the British Council in London asked to see the typescript of a novel accepted for publication. If I didn't withdraw the book, they then feared, they would never offer me another contract. I must choose. It wasn't a difficult choice.

Those professionally involved in the promulgation of culture must find books an awful nuisance.

✤

A SIX-YEAR-OLD boy in North Carolina is in trouble for planting a kiss on a girl in his primary school class, and has been made to miss a party and a colouring lesson. His offence is to have contravened the school's code prohibiting 'unwelcome sexual advances' (when questioned, the little girl said she hadn't asked for a kiss) and 'requests for sexual favours and other verbal or physical conduct of a sexual nature'. There were no previous convictions against him, sexual or otherwise.

So the guilt of adults is visited upon primary schoolchildren. What a lot of nasty little Jehovahs there are about. But the old Adam isn't so easily crushed. When asked if he intended to continue hugging people, the boy (he must have failed to take in the full import of the word 'sex') replied, 'Yep, sure!'

According to an American news item of a few years back, a feminist lobby devoted to correcting Puccini has come up with a new title for *Madame Butterfly*: 'The Court Martial of Lieutenant Pinkerton'. Fair enough. Except that Pinkerton doesn't rate star billing.

The new edition of a famous dictionary urges us to avoid the words 'handicap' and 'handicapped' because they evoke the hurtful image of disabled persons begging 'cap in hand' on the streets of Victorian London.

No doubt it is immaterial that (as lexicographers would know) the word 'handicap' appears to have originated in a game of chance, 'hand in cap', and was soon adopted by the racing fraternity: superior horses had to be handicapped to give the others a chance.

The term 'disabled' is too drastic to pass muster. Able to do nothing? Far from it, we often find. Some linguistic regulators favour 'physically challenged', but this suggests engagement in some form of pugilism. Best to forget images of Victorian London (supposing they had ever arisen) and politely disregard the dictionary.

Postscript. A Polish poet reading in London has been scolded by an Arts Council official for using the word 'crippled' in his own translation of one of his own poems. He should have said 'disabled'.

A thirteen-year-old girl reports in a letter to *The Times* how after she had mapped out a character study of Bottom on a computer—*A Midsummer Night's Dream* being an exam text—the machine took exception to her statement that Puck mischievously placed an ass's head on Bottom. It advised her, 'Avoid this offensive term. Consider revising.' Bottom plus ass was too much for its sense of propriety. (Yet computers can be down to earth when they feel like it. According to another letter in the same paper, when the writer ran the opening sentence of *Moby Dick*, the spell-checker suggested changing to 'Call me Fishmeal'.)

H. L. Mencken said of a certain author that he had 'a curious antipathy to the *mot juste*'. But a *mot*, no matter how *juste* you think it, can get you into dire trouble. Even a mildly indulgent fancy brings guilt with it: 'In my politically incorrect way I like to think of smiling inhabitants ready to welcome me' (a character on holiday in Switzerland, in Anita Brookner's *Altered States*). And we can all too easily be saddled with typesetters' *faux pas*; correcting proofs, I've just noticed a reference to an Egyptian gentleman's 'tarbrush' (a touch of the . . . ?); it was meant to be 'tarbush'.

In 1997 a baby competition in Hampshire, intended to raise money for hospitals, was cancelled after running for thirty years. The local health authority ruled that all babies were beautiful and therefore couldn't compete against one another.

The welcome sign at a prison crèche has been removed because the governor deems the words 'Jesus loves the little children' religiously provocative, in that a number of the prisoners are non-Christians. Not that anybody, whether inmates or visitors, had complained. The President of the Muslim College comments: 'As far as Muslims are concerned it is not offensive at all. We recognize Jesus as a prophet. If he loves children, that's fine by us.' Refreshing, that; normally, if people are told that something will offend them, they feel in honour bound to be offended.

Bibliophile: a lover of books. Paedophile: a lover of children. 'Suffer the little children to come unto me.' Jesus loves little children? If the man lives around here we must keep a close watch on our kiddies.

Is the press no more than an imprint of life, or is life only an imprint of the press? That was Karl Kraus's question back in 1914. We might fearfully ask the same question of our soap operas. Old *Coronation Street* has gone markedly downhill of late, as if aspiring to the depths of its brash rival, *EastEnders*. One lead-in (a trifle overly hopeful at the time) announced: 'Now, with love, lust, and jealousy, it's *Coronation Street*!'

A shining exception was Samir Rachid, the young Moroccan who brought joy into the life of doleful Deirdre; a decent, honourable, affectionate fellow, though for obscure reasons hated by Deirdre's ghastly daughter, Tracy, for whom nevertheless he was ready to sacrifice a kidney, she having ruined hers with drugs. Poor Samir, he alone was compatible, the only suitable boy at hand. On the way to the hospital he was beaten up by racist thugs (never brought to justice: there is little place for spoilsport policemen in the soaps) and died, a kidney still intact for graceless Tracy.

It would have been easy enough to keep Samir alive, perhaps winning the love or at least gratitude of his stepdaughter. Maybe he and Deirdre could have moved to Morocco, plainly a more salubrious spot than the suburbs of Manchester. (Deirdre's next great love will be a wooden-faced two-timing shop manager masquerading as an airline pilot.) But happiness wouldn't do; it's not an imprint of life, it's not an imprint of television. Samir had to go, swept away by that wearisome bully, the Zeitgeist; also—a foreigner at that—he was making the other inhabitants of the Street look shabby.

A few weeks later—art imitates art—Debbie, one of the few likeable characters in *EastEnders*, died in a road accident. The immediate effect was to make the others look a little less shabby than usual. They stood around speechless in the pub, or they moderated their language. They behaved well at the funeral.

It's a sad sign, when popular entertainment goes the way of highbrow art. How good it was to hear Bet Gilroy, then landlady of the Rovers Return, putting down a fanciful customer: 'Subconscious? It's a word that doesn't apply to any of my staff!' And nice—but so long ago—to hear Den Watts, then managing the Queen Victoria in *EastEnders*, putting down a pompous small-time journalist: 'Oh, writing for the *TLS* now, are you?' (Or did I dream it?)

Of late the Street has virtually become a no-go area, in part owing to the arrival of 'contemporary' low-life stereotypes (subspecies: 'neighbours from hell'). The actress who long played the genteel Mavis has walked out, love, lust, jealousy and miscellaneous mayhem having proved too much for her. (We must hope she has something put by.) Consequently the character Mavis had to be banished to a b. and b. in the Lake District, never to be seen again.

In *EastEnders*, during the run-up to Christmas 1996, the copulatory permutations and combinations soared to a new low. (All hidden from sight, as the time of transmission required, or in compliance with some primordial convention of the genre, or simply to spare what aesthetic susceptibilities we might happen to retain.) In the New Year, for a glorious moment, it looked as if half the cast would kill off the other half. Instead there ensued a feeble chorus of 'I never want to see you again!' A risky idea to put into the viewer's head. New Year 1998 brings more of the same. It's a rule in soap operas that characters never learn.

Other labour-saving turns of phrase indigenous to Albert Square are: 'We gotta talk', whereupon the person so addressed flounces off; 'What's that meant to mean?', when what's meant is plain as a pikestaff, and both parties flounce off; and 'I was out of order', the standard form of apology, whether for forgetting a birthday or inflicting grievous bodily harm on a nearest and dearest. Another rule is that characters never learn new expressions.

We sit in our room, in our home, in our locality, where we know none of the neighbours, we keep ourselves to ourselves, they keep themselves to themselves. And we all watch the soap operas, where everybody knows everybody else, and everybody is wrangling with everybody else, lying to them, spying on them, traducing them, cheating them. We are fascinated by this revelation of community life. We are very glad we have no share in it.

AN Indian professor asks for a contribution to a proposed book on teaching *The Waste Land* in sundry lands and circumstances.

Alexandria, 1947–50. The question hardly arose in day-to-day teaching despite the local attraction of 'Falling towers/Jerusalem Athens Alexandria'. The students had more pressing concerns, social, political, falling finances. *Macbeth*, *Silas Marner* and a few Wordsworth lyrics were about as far as we got. (There must have been some reason why *Antony and Cleopatra* wasn't on the syllabus; possibly it was feared the play might arouse unsuitable passions. An Arabic version of *Romeo and Juliet* briskly rendered Juliet's lament, 'O Romeo, Romeo! wherefore art thou Romeo?' as *'Enta fein, Roméo?'*: Where are you, Romeo?) We must have taught some Eliot in the final year —always rather depleted, as students vanished into their villages, or prison, or madhouse—since at the time I noted down a creative misreading in an exam paper: '. . . a Lovesong of Prue Frock about a man and a woman getting into bed together and getting out again. This was never done in literature before. And that is why Mr Eliot is important.'

Japan, 1953–6. The poem was invariably received with an enthusiasm which surpassed understanding, or dispensed with it, as though absorbed into the mind by some virtually non-intellectual process of osmosis. The poem was seen as validating a then common state of mind. To quote from a reference of mine (1955): '*The Waste Land* has been moved from Europe, rather in the fashion of "The Ghost Goes West", and set down in the Far East. Admittedly it fits rather neatly—an English friend remarked that "What are the roots that clutch, what branches grow/Out of this stony rubbish?" might well have been said of postwar Tokyo.' As if in confirmation, one of my women students accounted thus for the current popularity of such writers as Eliot, Sartre and Graham Greene: 'Their darkness and sarcasm and negative spirit have attracted attention in Japan, for it is natural to be welcomed these points in absence of mind after war.' It wasn't mind that was absent so much as *awaré*, the traditional sadness of things, that was present. One wondered—Edmund Blunden did, if I remember correctly—whether by teaching the poem one wasn't adding gratuitously to the misery or at least melancholy of the nation during those postwar years. In retrospect I don't think one did much harm.

Thailand, 1957–9. Out of the question. The relentless nice-mindedness of the young people, and their distaste for strong and tiring emotions ('It is too hot to think about them'), precluded such grim, demanding stuff. In this country the head is the seat of the soul, and you take care what you put into it. In any case good Buddhists, as they all appeared to be, had arrived at the heart of the matter long before. 'Burning burning burning burning.'

Singapore, 1960–70. The subsequent history of the country might lead one to expect a radical rejection of the poem as negative thinking and a symptom of Western decay, but in fact it generated immense interest. English literature was *for* these young people—they were pretty well at home with the language—but not necessarily *about* them. (Not an unhealthy attitude, it must be granted.) What most drew them was the expressive imagery, the dramatic quality, the excitement of 'I think we are in rats' alley . . .', the jazzy interjection of 'O O O O that Shakespeherian Rag', those naughty 'exploring hands': the poem's very difference from the poetry they had studied in school. Hence it made them feel grown-up; a feeling by no means abated if they claimed to detect a degree of exaggeration (often present in Western writing), of 'going too far'—in this unconsciously echoing George Orwell's comment that Eliot had achieved 'the difficult feat of making modern life out to be worse than it is'.

Leamington Spa, me. Not teaching but learning. The poem aroused a puzzled fascination, not unlike that of the Singapore students: admiration for the technical innovations, the scene-shifting, the filmic aspect ('bats with baby faces in the violet light'), the pungency, the un-romanticness. All this along with growing doubts concerning the social inferences, the totality of the disillusionment (Eliot's reference to the poem as 'just a piece of rhythmical grumbling' would have struck me as both modest and disingenuous), and in particular the low-life section in 'A Game of Chess' ('What you get married for if you don't want children?'), which to me, for all its clever ventriloquism, smacked of unfeeling, uncomprehending condescension. With the passing years I find an uneasy, vacillating preference for the *Four Quartets* setting in. Not so surprising. In a comment on the ending of the Second Part of *Faust,* Goethe surmised that in old age we all become mystics. Perhaps that's going too far; but if in age we are still to have a state of mind, it will have to be a different one. Old men may be as irritable as the tiger in the tiger-pit, losing their sight, smell, hearing etc., but they can still be explorers in a modest way.

※

PEOPLE tell us of the richness—compared with the poverty of standard English—of this or that little-known language or dialect spoken by some remote, sheltered or tiny community. Of course such languages are rich: no one spends them.

Irritation aside, we feel sorrow, we feel a chill, at the passing of any language. In January 1996 Red Thunder Cloud died at 76, the last person to speak the language of the Catawba tribe; in his latter years the only one to understand him was his dog. And Dr David Dalby, a champion of 'small' languages, tells of an 87-year-old African woman crooning to herself in Bikya, a tongue she alone understands, while not far away a father and his son are the only people left speaking Bishuo.

I think of Richard Wilbur's moving poem of loss, 'To the Etruscan Poets':

> Dream fluently, still brothers, who when young
> Took with your mothers' milk the mother tongue,
>
> In which pure matrix, joining world and mind,
> You strove to leave some line of verse behind
>
> Like a fresh track across a field of snow,
> Not reckoning that all could melt and go.

'I like our language . . . Who cannot dress it well, want wit, not words.' George Herbert got it right. Not so a certain reviewer (or typesetter): 'Castaneda's voracity has been often questioned.' (It might be questioned whether the guru in question didn't sometimes bite off more than he could chew.) Likewise the managing director of a publishing house who assures us in a press release that the firm's medium size 'allows a flexibility and friendliness that larger conglomerated companies mitigate against'. In publishing circles 'backlist' has become a verb: 'I'm afraid your book isn't likely to backlist' (i.e. it is listing badly). But it's rather pleasing to envisage politicians 'towing the party line' instead of being towed by it. In another press item 'Cannon X' is an excusable error, the clergyman's style of preaching having just been described as 'explosive'.

A writer in *The Times*, discussing the nuisance of crowing cockerels, has recommended 'canonization'. More humane, one supposes, than caponization.

An erratum slip in a book of 1945 marked a different sort of mistake: 'Page 29, delete "unfrocked by the all-knowing bishop", and substitute "suspended, at his own request".'

The clergy are constantly in trouble. This Australian verse comes from the nineteenth century:

> The preacher quoted, and the cranks
>   Among his congregation smiled,
> 'How sharper than a serpent's thanks
>   It is to have a toothless child!'

> He saw he erred, his eye grew wild,
>   He frowned upon the mirthful ranks:
> 'How toothless than a serpent's child
>   It is to have a sharper's thanks!'

'That anti-feminist backlash when postwar women were exalted to devote their lives to housewifely domesticity . . .': in a reference to

Betty Friedan's *The Feminine Mystique*. Was it 'exhorted', maimed in transmission, or an incorrect thought peeping slyly out?

Attacking a proposal that teachers could be sacked if their pupils performed badly in exams, the general secretary of the National Association of Schoolmasters and Union of Women Teachers declares that 'To call this measure Victorian or Draconian is an insult to Victoria and Dracula.' No one proposes to sack him.

A letter in *The Times* offers a nice addendum. A local (Cornish) paper has lamented that these days the night sky can be clearly seen only by people who 'live in the Styx'.

To add to the list of 'literally's used to mean the opposite, a correspondent conveys this instance: 'He literally charmed the pants off every girl he met.' (Mind you, with so much magic realism about . . .) The *New Fowler's Modern English Usage* gives some ripe examples, including 'And with his eyes he literally scoured the corners of the cell': V. Nabokov, 1960, and (borderline) 'They [supermarkets] can literally play God, even to the point of sending food back to the genetic drawing-board for a redesign': *Guardian*, 1995.

A reader has pointed out some garbled quotations in a new book on Byron. E.g., 'Hobhouse recorded in his diary: "dangers and fears by way of supper"', when what Hobhouse actually recorded was 'oranges and pears by way of supper'. Literary scholars have such inflamed imaginations.

In Singapore my wife worked briefly for Reuters, translating news items into French for dissemination in Vietnam and Cambodia. One item, concerning the test flight of a new plane, reported that the temperature remained constant throughout the flight. In transmission *vol* turned into *viol*: 'the temperature remained constant throughout the rape'.

I see in a recent scholarly publication that a book of mine, *A Mania for Sentences*, features as *A Man for Sentences*. Not quite what Flaubert's mother said, but I guess it will pass. In the *New York Review*'s notes on contributors, another book appears as *The Alluring: An Essay on Irony*. No one wants to bother with a Problem. People nod off halfway through the title!

Some typesetters don't take well to being corrected. One of them, engaged on a military history, represented a battle-scarred general as 'bottle-scarred'. This was put right in proof, whereupon the adjective reappeared as 'battle-scared'. (Perhaps it's clichés they don't care for.)
    Printers being of more account than princes, it was one of them, *c.*1702, who gave the Psalmist to complain, 'Printers have persecuted me without a cause.'

I was put out this week to read in detective novels by exceptionally literate authors of (a) 'the poet Keates' and (b) a police inquiry which 'illicited nothing new'. But cheered to come across this saying in a novel by the Australian, Jon Cleary: 'They'd steal the bridle off of a nightmare.'

According to the press, a new MP, Labour's youngest member ever, has no office in the Commons and nowhere to live in her Watford constituency. 'I'm wandering around with all my wordly goods in a couple of carrier bags.' Enough to make a maiden speech, we trust.

The Before Midnight Scholar (in Chinese, 'The Prayer Mat of Flesh') is a seventeenth-century novel which follows the ancient recipe in which lashings of naughtiness are topped with a sprinkling of repentance. It ends with a moral: 'From this it can be seen that everyone in this world can aspire to Buddhahood. It is only wordly desires which shackle them, and prevent them from escaping from the vanity of the world and reaching salvation on the other side.' Many of us will have had the same thought.

Engulfed in atmospheric interference, this poor soul is thoroughly confused. 'The world was misprinted its first day./In the beginning was the lord'; and the beginning was in the Book of Genocide. Correcting proofs in a dream, he finds he has written 'Patriots always stand for the National Anathema', and 'Seven Hypes of Ambiguity'. He's relieved that his misprints make such sense, but reflects: 'A pity my books/are kept so plain by too much meaning.' (Peter Porter, 'A Bag of Pressmints'.)

> 'In the beginning was the Word', I see.
> I'm stuck already! Who can counsel me?
> The *Word*? That high I cannot rate it,
> Some other way I must translate it . . .
> The spirit helps! I see how it should read,
> And boldly write, 'In the beginning was the *Deed*'

—Professor Faust in his study, turning St John's Greek into German.

Goethe said, 'When I come across a misprint I always think something new has been invented.'

❧

'LIFE isn't a television aerial.' The words leap off the glum pages of a Czech novel I'm plodding through.

A brilliant image. Life's not passive, but proactive. It's not scheduled, it doesn't come pre-programmed from some huge transmitter in the sky. It comes from within, it has its limits, but it's ours. We don't have to be voyeurs; we are actors, not audience. Masses, yes, but not mass produced, not other people's reconstituted pictures; neither sitcoms nor documentaries. For better or for worse we are driven by more than tiny electric impulses. We receive but what we give (and take). Life is . . .

Much refreshed, I turn back to the book. Good Lord! What it says is 'Life isn't a television serial', adding tritely that everything comes to an end one day.

Creative misprision, you might call it. I was reading rather better than the author wrote.

❧

BY virtue of 'the specific density of linguistic autonomy', George Steiner has said, 'language is the adversary of translation'. He cites Ortega y Gasset on the peculiar sadness translators feel, caused by their perception of the inadequacies and likely transience of their labours, and adduces a 'deeper source of malaise': 'The process of mastering comprehension and of "transportation" (the word carries sombre political-judicial overtones) can leave the original text lessened and inert.'

True, language is a devil, and the conjunction of two languages can be pandemonium. But surely the comprehension of anything worth comprehending (and translating) isn't going to lessen it. As for overtones, they are the stock-in-trade of the smutty comedian, and the rest of us will know how to keep them in their place.

A natural but bad habit of intellectuals is to make what is difficult sound impossible. Actually Steiner treasures translation—'supreme translation, which is no more frequent than eminent poetry'—as 'the counter-statement to Babel'.

'In translating one must on no account get involved in hand-to-hand fighting with the foreign language,' Goethe warned. 'One must go all the way to the untranslatable, and respect it; for precisely therein lie the value and the character of every language.'

Translation is a very odd business; and being a business, it can't always afford too much respect. Time is money; generally not much of it. Yet occasionally respect takes an unexpected form. In 1960 Paul Scott wrote to me in Singapore to ask if I could provide a rendering in elegant Chinese characters of the title of his forthcoming novel, *The Chinese Love Pavilion*, for use on the jacket. I asked an elderly gentleman scholar, by name Chao Tai, renowned for his fine calligraphy, if he would be kind enough to oblige. A few days later he presented me with an inscription corresponding to 'Love Pavilion', explaining that with the best will in the world he simply couldn't introduce the epithet 'Chinese'. The words were Chinese, the plain implication was that the love pavilion was therefore Chinese, and to have spelt it out would have grated unbearably on the sensibility. This was fine by Paul Scott, though unfortunately I had omitted to indicate which way up the characters went, and further correspondence ensued.

(The Japanese are always telling us about 'Japanese saké', albeit this wine is uniquely and solely Japanese. But then, they are addressing foreigners. Also they produce a very tolerable whisky, and may have it in mind that one day the Scots will retaliate with a Scottish saké.)

Another of Goethe's shrewd sayings has it that 'Translators are like busy pimps extolling the surpassing charms of some half-veiled beauty. They excite an irresistible desire for the original.'

While busily pimping—along with my wife, I hasten to say—on a light revision of the Scott Moncrieff/Terence Kilmartin translation of Proust's novel, I was taken aback to read that towards the end of a musical soirée someone remarked that they ought to bid their hostess goodbye: 'We can't take French leave.' That's a good English idiom, and it's nice when you can render one idiom so directly by another. But this is hardly what you would expect to hear from a Frenchman. Proust has the good French idiom, *partir à l'anglaise*, which we turned into 'We can't slip away, English fashion'.

Reading more closely or suspiciously than is normal, we were puzzled by a description of the Balbec church porch and its representation of the pregnant Virgin and the attendant midwife with a 'bandaged arm'. What intriguing story lay behind that arm? Had the midwife been bitten by a resentful baby, or clawed by some mother in the pains of childbirth? We sought out pictures of churches which might have served as models for Balbec, and for accounts of any apposite legend. Without success. So back to the word *bandé*, which did indeed mean 'bandaged'—but could also signify 'outstretched'. (And hence has featured in indecent slang.) And that was it: the incredulous midwife—how could a virgin be pregnant?—had stretched out her arm to feel the womb.

Scott Moncrieff is unsurpassable in aesthetic matters, descriptions of works of art and natural phenomena, but deficient or quaint in his dealings with idiomatic passages, as Kilmartin noted, and particularly the language of low life, whether through squeamishness or ignorance. His delicate reference to the 'swooning mouth' of a woman during the act of love we toned down to the literal 'convulsed mouth'. Among scurrilous allusions to M. de Charlus appearing in the press was the sobriquet 'Gaillard d'arrière', literally 'Quarterdeck', but carrying sexual connotations. In Scott Moncrieff this appeared mildly as 'Jolly Sailor'; we changed it to 'Jolly Rear Admiral', for reasons I need not dwell on.

Elsewhere we corrected 'a cat and dog life', a misunderstanding of a French idiom, to 'living it up', and modernized 'pilled' (by the Jockey Club) to 'blackballed', and 'floater' to (the original) 'gaffe'. Strangely, a woman at a party was said to be on the point of death; Proust described her as 'foaming at the mouth', not because she was terminally ill, but because she was only too alive and perpetually raging against other people. Revisers, lowly pedants, will peruse their texts ploddingly, mistrustfully, grudgingly. When in a metaphorical passage I came on a pair of ships leaving port for unknown destinations 'with a joyous crackling of flames', alarm bells began to sound. A fire at sea is scarcely joyous: what was Proust thinking of with his 'claquement joyeux de flammes'? A barbecue in the galley? Ah, but 'flammes' can signify 'oriflammes'—and what was crackling or snapping in the breeze were pennants.

In the second Pléiade edition of *À la recherche du temps perdu* a pronoun changes sex usefully, a niece more pertinently becomes a mother, and several new passages clear up long-standing (though perhaps rarely noticed) mysteries. Best of all are these ten new words, lost and regained: 'Profonde Albertine que je voyais dormir et qui était morte'. How fine, how right, that on the penultimate page of the work, as the narrator brings to a close his musing on Time, there should be this sudden apparition: 'Profound Albertine, whom I saw sleeping and who was dead.'

'The majority of publishers,' says Terry Hale, director of the British Centre for Literary Translation, 'still treat translators like casual labourers.' And Alain de Botton adds that, like waiters, they draw our attention only when something goes wrong. (The EU interpreter who turned a remark about the need for 'la sagesse normande' into 'the need for Norman Wisdom' is readily exonerated, with the tiniest of smiles.) Translators are customarily such quiet and modest creatures, and I mention these few translational curiosities purely to enlarge the skimpy anecdotage attached to the subject.

No, not purely. Goethe complained to Henry Crabb Robinson that the critics failed to perceive that Werther praised Homer while he retained his senses and Ossian only when he was going mad. 'But reviewers do not notice such things.' None of the reviews of the revised Proust, published in 1992 as *In Search of Lost Time*, cited any of the changes. Reviewers do not notice such things.

It can be disconcerting to work with the author of what you are translating when he is pretty well up in your language. He knows what he means better than you do; he always seems to be right, and you shamingly wrong. No such trouble with Proust or Goethe.

And yet, hearteningly, the business goes on. A contributor's note in the *Times Literary Supplement* runs, 'He is currently completing a translation of Genesis.' With the author's help? At the end of *God: A Biography* Jack Miles lists the names of some forty people whose help he gratefully acknowledges, in alphabetical order, including God.

On some translations by Helmut Winter

Reading them against the old originals—
Back then, you think, you had some talent,
Almost lyrical, a gentle sadness,
Here and there a word not quite expected,
Now and then a dash of simple humour . . .
Ah well, sadness comes expensive these days,
The unexpected takes too large a toll,
Nothing's simple enough for simple humour,
While lyricism faded long ago . . .
What's left? These phrases in a foreign tongue.

In his late seventies, when reading something in French, Goethe remarked to himself that the man spoke quite cleverly, one wouldn't have put it in any other way. Looking more closely at the passage, he realized it was a translation from his own writings.

TWENTY-FOUR years after my (not wholly voluntary but no doubt overdue) departure, my former students clubbed together to fly me out to Singapore, into a tip-top hotel, no expense spared, for a Grand Reunion and a number of smaller ones. In prospect this was somewhat unnerving; in the event, a magical time.

Having become more prosperous than its founding fathers could have envisaged, the country was now looking about for a past, something extra to pearlers, pirates and entrepreneurs, to go with its shining present. Was it possible—the immodest or comical thought occurred—that I was part of its history, if no more than a tiny naysaying hiccup? At all events, one of my students was now Chief

Executive Officer of the National Heritage Board. And another was Minister for Home Affairs, a fact so discomfiting to the local newspaper, devoted of old to watching its p's and q's, that all it dared term me was 'controversial', an epithet which no doubt had earlier been used of Stamford Raffles.

Externally Singapore had changed drastically. Where once shophouses had hugged the earth there were tower blocks, often luxurious within; Orchard Road was a succession of famous names: fashion houses, jewellers, perfumeries; the island had even grown in size by the addition of land won from the sea. But the students were unchanged; they seemed as young as when I had left them, though a good deal better off. (One wants one's students to do well, doesn't one? Would one wish to have them languishing in prison?) My one-time secretary, now a grandmother, was as meekly bossy as ever, and —now we approach the point of this inconsequential tale—she had arranged for me to call on the erstwhile Minister of Culture, now in retirement from affairs of state: someone with whom I had crossed swords, or wooden daggers.

Magdalene, a sweet-natured creature, wanted everybody to love everybody else, and was perhaps moved by the secretarial urge to see an ancient file closed for good. I groaned, I declared petulantly that I had no intention of visiting the fellow who had threatened me with hard words and deportation. Then shame overcame me; they had been so very generous and kind, surely I could make a little effort. Finally, in the privacy of my hotel bedroom, I rang the Minister's secretary, who expressed delight and put me through to his master. The Minister had certainly aged. Without preliminaries, he asked whether I was aware that men had developed from animals. When I admitted cautiously to an acquaintance with the theory, he explained that he was engaged on a great philosophical work. Good, I said brightly, it was good to have an interest in one's—er—leisure years. 'My research is this: since men came after animals, I am asking what will come after men.' Women, I ventured, with the lack of circumspection that had landed me in hot water all those years ago. (Also because his party had always been stiffly disdainful of the sex.) The philosopher ignored the suggestion, and rambled on about the time and thought he had given to this momentous and strangely neglected question. When I could get a word in, I remarked diplomatically on the youthful appearance of my sometime students, wondering whether it wasn't due to—I couldn't bring myself to credit governmental policies with it—due to something in the air. This too he brushed aside, and the conversation petered out in laboured civilities. The philosopher wanted to get back to his philosophy; I hoped for a little lie-down.

It struck me later that the Minister may not have known who it was he was speaking with. Still, honour had been satisfied; it was easily satisfied. And Magdalene blessed me with a warm smile and a pat on the shoulder. 'You did the right thing, Prof.'

Perhaps in the end

Perhaps in the end it's simply I enjoy a place
where the politics are simple and clear-cut,
or virtually non-existent, and all civic biddings
issue from stern daughters of the Voice of God
(if literally speaking sons). Maybe in the end
I'm seduced by law and order, clean streets and loos,
creature comforts, an air of overbearing health
(I'm just about the only smoker furtively about).
I like the dresses, I like the women wearing them,
the men are mannerly, and still appreciate a joke
(joking's my visa, chief purpose of my visit).
But intellectual anguish? One can have too much,
and 'face', that fiat, keeps a brave face on things.
Nice to be exempt from sad or sick biographies!
And human rights? There's always one, the right
to keep your head down. I knew these people when
they were poor, I'm glad to see them prosperous.
An earthly paradise!—Eden was rather boring
till the Lord reached out for his rattan. Boredom's
not that bad, the better often buggers up the good.

Poor and downtrodden's one thing, rich and browbeaten
something else. These days my bones ache so, I'm not
inclined to play the snake. And don't forget, I'm just
a foreigner (as once the Voice of God rubbed in),
one who can always cut and run when times get tough.
And in the end what's death itself except decamping?

※

'FOR many, the acquisition of riches has not made an end of troubles, but an alteration': Epicurus. Mammon is a busy god, currently rubbing his hands over the National Lottery, and the Church is right to keep an eye on him. But not a tendentious eye. In deploring the way money can go to the head of the common man, it should avoid any suggestion that money is safe with those used to it, those whom God, as it were, has called to it.

But are we to endure every week for the rest of our lives the insensate howling and screeching that attend the BBC's broadcast of the National Lottery draw? The cat—totally unresponsive to television screams of children at play, sports fans, wrangling couples, demonstrations, mortal agony, and orgasm—leaves the room as soon as the first ball begins its descent.

You can be sure that should beings from outer space arrive on earth, majestic, beautiful to behold, radiating indisputable goodness and grace, bearing priceless gifts, simple and compelling lessons in love, compassion and charity—you can be sure they wouldn't meet with anything approaching the waves of excitement, the cries of unbounded joy, that greet the Lottery twice every week.

A predominant feature of the news consists in sums of money: salaries, bonuses, law suits, compensation, settlements, negative equity, fraud, betting on the Grand National, transfer fees for footballers, street value of illicit drugs, Arts Council grants to theatres, publishers' advances, the cost of new prisons, of the Millennium Dome, of a classroom, of a hospital bed. Our society may not be outstandingly literate but it is conspicuously numerate.

Money is the most sheeplike thing on earth. We are all fond of sheep. Money follows money slavishly, it loves to flock. If, like the lemming, it charges off a cliff, it lands on its feet or its fat fleece. More plainly than in the theological sense of the saying, falling furthers the flight in it. 'Debt is the optimism of Americans': James Buchan.

Money is so simple, so easy to believe in, whether you have it or not. Money is the only sure sign that a person matters. It is not subjective, it is gloriously objective. Beauty counts for something, but it's only skin-deep, whereas money permeates flesh, blood and bone, and is in the eye of *every* beholder. We like simplicity.

Nothing new about this, of course, apart from its erection into a self-evidently just law. There's an aura of innocence and incredulity about Dickens's amused indignation in 1864: 'Traffic in Shares is the one thing to have to do with in this world. Have no antecedents, no established character, no cultivation, no ideas, no manners; have Shares . . . Where does he come from? Shares. Where is he going to? Shares. What are his tastes? Shares. Has he any principles? Shares . . . Perhaps he never of himself achieved success in anything, never originated anything, never produced anything! Sufficient answer to all: Shares.'

To the young Jenkins, in Anthony Powell's *A Question of Upbringing*, money was a 'mysterious entity, of which one had heard so much and so often without grasping more than that its ownership was desirable and its lack inconvenient'; he came to understand that 'its possession can become as much part of someone as the nose on the face'. As Philip Larkin noted, 'Clearly money has something to do with life.'

However modest we are, we may find a little difficulty in appreciating how some business executives can earn in a few months as much as we hope to earn in a lifetime of full employment. We may not be persuaded by the claim that such individuals are extremely rare, universally sought after, and hence worth every penny, for there can't be that scarcity of financial talent, genius if you will, around.

But to show one's scepticism on this score is to be charged with 'the politics of envy'. What a mean and ludicrous expression! It echoes that other exotic accusation, 'penis envy'—to which, Frank Cioffi has remarked, Freud was committed 'willy-nilly (or maybe I had better say *nolens volens*)'—and hence insinuates that one can't support a family, one is consumed with impotent resentment, one isn't a proper man. It also suggests that one is a politician.

There's another side to the question, it seems. Drawing on the medical journals ever alert to the latest maladies of body and soul, the *Oxford Dictionary of New Words* directs our attention to a psychiatric disorder affecting the rich and characterized by feelings of malaise, unworthiness, boredom and guilt.

> Pity the wealthy—
> Struck down by affluenza,
> They feel quite poorly.

Mr Podsnap was convinced that the poor will always be with us—by divine dispensation. This pious consideration didn't deter him from thinking the subject an odious one.

We can't afford to make the poor less poor. But we could surely find a way of making the rich a little less rich, which ought to have much the same effect. (Besides assuaging the condition mentioned above.) Except, it appears, we can't afford to. The rich are always with us.

Behavioural issues.
   Peculation continues to thrive. The chief executive of the Student Loans Company has been found milking the coffers. 'Whisky, cigars and tickets to pop concerts bought at taxpayers' expense,' says the press. He has been on sick leave for the past three months or so; so he's sick, he's not criminal. But apparently fit enough to work in some unspecified capacity in a Scottish restaurant. (Cooking the books?) His deputy pleads that it wasn't a large-scale swindle, as swindles go, but 'more a behavioural issue'. Lovely expression; it would be wasted on a squalid shoplifter. The Education Secretary assures us that no compensation will be paid to the man for the loss of his £75,000 p.a. job.
   A 'distinguished academic' and deputy chief executive of the Welsh Joint Education Committee, earning £50,000 p.a., is charged with false accounting in that he submitted claims for travel expenses, some 300 first-class rail fares, amounting to over £21,000, to attend education meetings in London, whereas in reality he visited galleries and museums. The defence maintains that the man is 'a respected and erudite academic', and no furtive affairs, gambling, alcohol or drug-taking were involved. Rather than sit through useless meetings, he chose to spend the time in such undeniably educational places as the Tate Gallery and the Natural History Museum. 'Almost unworldly in the naïvety of his outlook', he is 'a donnish intellectual and he has been cocooned in academia for most of his adult life'.
   An academic exercise. Define and comment on the following terms: 'distinguished', 'respected', 'erudite', 'unworldly', 'naïvety', 'donnish', 'intellectual', 'cocooned', 'academia'.

A shocking thing to admit, but I begin to value my correspondents according to whether the stamps on their envelopes are cancelled or not. A handy tip picked up in some Grub Street tavern: don't peel the stamp from the envelope, peel the envelope away from the stamp.

Unhappily all those letters offering to help me with my financial planning are franked—no retrievable stamps to help me with my financial planning.

※

A LONDON priest is said to have warned his congregation of scouts that he was about to tell them a parable. 'You know what a parable is? It's a heavenly story with no earthly meaning.'

In a vineyard there is a fig tree which has failed to bear fruit for three years running. The owner instructs his gardener to cut it down, for it is only encumbering the earth. The gardener asks him to spare the tree for another year, while he digs in manure around it. If it then bears fruit, so much the better; if not, it will be chopped down.

The parable has puzzled readers. It can't merely be urging that a man should be given a second chance to redeem himself. The fig tree has already had three chances. Something must have got lost in the telling. Perhaps Luke was hurrying on to the healing of the arthritic woman, a matter of more general interest. But if you transpose the story to the publishing scene it makes perfect sense.

The managing director, who has just come from a painful meeting with the accountants, observes that some book hasn't been selling for the past three years, and it had better be removed from the list, thus making room for a more profitable item. The editor who originally took the book on pleads for a year's respite, during which he will do his best to procure a puff on local radio, have a word with Waterstone's, spread a little fertilizer around. If these efforts don't bear fruit during the next twelve months, the book will get the chop.

No need for an explicit conclusion. We know what will happen.

More puzzling, and more troubling since it features not as a parable but as an incident in the life of Jesus, is a story recounted by both Matthew and Mark. Jesus was hungry one morning; seeing a fig tree some distance away, he approached it, but found no fruit there. Whereupon he cursed it: 'Let no fruit grow on thee henceforward for ever.' And it promptly withered away.

Jesus then took the opportunity to attach a lesson, telling his amazed disciples that if they had faith they could do what he had done to the fig tree, they could even persuade a mountain to cast itself into the sea. Surely less than convincing? One feels aggrieved for the poor tree. Indeed, the incident provoked Cyril Connolly into taking Jesus to task as a petulant man, cursing the tree out of sheer spite just because he was 'very partial' to figs.

Alain agrees that to curse a fig tree for barrenness *when it wasn't the season for figs* (a pertinent detail supplied by Mark: 'for the time of figs was not yet') is unacceptable, adding that one's first reaction is to try to find out 'what witless copyist or misformed letters' could have been responsible for the damaging admission that figs couldn't be expected at the time. But wait: one shouldn't seek to change a text before striving earnestly to understand it. And it comes to Alain that the question is not of literal fig trees but of humans, human fig trees, those in positions of power who say, the time is not ripe . . . , circumstances do not permit . . . , there are no funds available . . . , the office is closing for the weekend . . . , the computers are down . . . , perhaps, next year . . . (Cf. Proverbs 3:28, 'Say not unto thy neighbour, Go, and come again, and tomorrow I will give.')

This is 'the order of Caesar, which always invokes and always will invoke necessity against justice'; and this is what is cursed in us. So, a true parable after all. In which case perhaps the innocent fig tree did not die in vain.

A tale bearing on the magical properties of the written word occurs in a book by John Wilkins, a founder member of the Royal Society. A slave is sent by his master to deliver a basket of figs and a letter. On the way, being very partial to figs, he eats a large number of them. The recipient, having read the letter, suspects the slave of stealing the figs. The slave protests that the piece of paper is a false and lying witness. Later the slave is sent again, with figs and a letter indicating how many figs there should be. This time too he devours a large part of them, but only after burying the letter temporarily under a stone, so that it wouldn't see what he was doing. Being accused none the less, he confesses the truth, marvelling ruefully at the divinity of the piece of paper.

The Chinese poet Ai Qing tells of a man who was eager to hunt and besought a professional hunter to teach him how to shoot birds. The hunter instructed him in the characteristics of various birds and how to aim and fire his gun, which happened to be a good one. The man considered this was enough, and hurried into the woods, but as soon as he raised the gun, all the birds flew away.

When he complained, his teacher asked whether he would prefer to shoot a bird that couldn't fly. To tell the truth, that would suit him fine. So the teacher told him to go home, draw a bird on a sheet of cardboard, hang the cardboard on a tree, and then take aim. That way he couldn't miss.

But he did. Perhaps (he said) because he had drawn the bird too small or had stood too far away from it.

Professing to admire his determination, the teacher took thought and advised him to use a larger sheet of cardboard, and shoot at it from whatever distance he fancied. Without drawing a bird on it? Yes. But then he would merely be shooting at a piece of cardboard! Ah, said the teacher solemnly, just keep firing at the cardboard, and when you have used all your bullets, draw a bird round each hole, as many birds as there are holes.

A parable, surely, with much deep wisdom inside it. But since, unlike the one about the fig tree, it makes a good story, read as reading, let's not gild the lily. A bird in the hand . . .

A fellow called Luigi volunteered for service the moment war broke out. This was because he had an enemy, Alberto, whom for personal reasons he desired to kill. It was explained to him repeatedly that war wasn't like that, it was the enemy he was supposed to kill, not an individual called Alberto, and he had to go and fight where they ordered him. He wasn't happy about this. He killed a lot of people, and won a lot of medals, but he hadn't killed Alberto. So all those people had died for nothing.

The enemy surrendered. Luigi went round the defeated country, giving his medals to the wives and children of the dead. Then one day he bumped into Alberto, and killed him. He was tried for murder and hanged. At his trial he insisted that he had done it to quieten his conscience, but no one listened.

This fable was written in 1943, when Italo Calvino was twenty. He said then that fables were written in times of oppression, when one had to wrap up one's thoughts, and once things had changed, fables would no longer be necessary. But he continued to write them.

The point is pretty clear, there. Another of Calvino's fables, barely a printed page long, has to do with a town where everything was forbidden, except the game we call tipcat. The various prohibitions had been brought in one at a time, for what sounded like good reasons, and the townspeople had grown used to them. They spent the whole day playing tipcat.

One day it dawned on the town's authorities, the constables as they were called, that there was no real reason, or no longer any reason, why everything should be forbidden, and the people were informed that they could do whatever they wished, they were free to return to all those delightful pursuits so long denied them. Fine, said the people, but they weren't interested. They were busy playing tipcat. How exasperating! Not to say ungrateful. The constables thought of a solution: all they had to do was ban tipcat, tipcat alone. They did, and the people rose up and killed the lot of them.

The moral isn't quite so plain here. Maybe: you can forbid this and prohibit that, and get clean away with it. Then, perhaps with the very best intentions, you revoke some trivial but treasured right (like game-shows on television, or planting trees, or free care for the sick and elderly), and that's the end of you.

In dread of the Relieving Officer, 'the Parish', the Poorhouse, Betty Higden scrapes a living by selling trifles to ladies. Her dignified demeanour, 'bright eyes and hopeful speech', and clean clothes, give rise to the notion that, considering her station, she is really quite well-to-do. 'As making a comfortable provision for its subject which costs nobody anything, this class of fable has long been popular.' (*Our Mutual Friend*.)

Then there are those incidents or scenes, more or less vaguely yet stubbornly emblematic, known in the trade as 'epiphanies'. Walking into her office in the University of Singapore one day, I found my secretary frozen in an unnatural posture, as if playing the party game of Statues, one hand held against her head, the other stretched out over the waste-paper basket. 'What's this, Magdalene?' She had been reading the department library's copy of *Lady Chatterley's Lover*, the old expurgated version, when a fearful thought struck her. She rang her confessor, an Irish priest, who told her, 'Cast it away, my daughter, at once!' 'But'—she spoke in baffled anguish—'I couldn't do it, Prof. It's university property!' I took the book from her clenched fingers and restored it to the library. She was a devout Catholic, and also a pragmatic Chinese, torn between two conflicting codes.

In *The Sickness unto Death* Kierkegaard relates an anecdote of a peasant who came barefoot to town with his produce, and did so well that he treated himself to a fine pair of shoes with stockings to match. And treated himself to drink, as well. On the way home he lay down in the middle of the street and fell asleep. A carriage came along, and the coachman shouted to him to move aside or he would drive over his legs. Waking up, the peasant peered at his new shoes and stockings, and grunted: 'Go ahead, they aren't my legs.'

Fairly certainly a parable. And, I wouldn't wonder, signifying . . . But enough; remember the words of Solomon: 'As a thorn goeth up into the hand of a drunkard, so is a parable in the mouth of fools.'

Even so. 'I find my own biography in every fable I read': Emerson.

SHORT c.v. of a spy. Teaching abroad, he is asked by a diplomat, a junior one he suspects, to report on the views and attitudes of his colleagues at the university. 'They'll trust you.' He rather likes the sound of this. 'But I might—er—have views of my own, which could—er—affect my judgement . . .' 'We shall make the appropriate adjustment.' He doesn't altogether like the sound of that.

Some while later—he thought they had forgotten him—he is called in for debriefing, no less.

Are they against war in general? In particular, having recently lost one. Would you say they are pacifists? To a militant degree. What do they say about the bombings? They say they understand. Are they resentful concerning the Occupation? They find it well-meaning, with minor reservations such as excessive disinfectant in the water-supply. Do they display communist leanings? Clobbered so thoroughly, they lean in a number of directions. Do they ever mention their former leaders? They seem to consider them unmentionable. What is their opinion of democracy? They regard it as a very interesting theory. When you eat and drink with them, what do they talk about? Food and drink. Are you aware of any secret societies? Every family. Do they show admiration for our country? For our literature. What foreign writers do they favour? Those they wrote their theses on. Do you know of any writings in private circulation? A cyclostyled account of the structure of modification with a class 1 word as the head and its immediate constituents; a copiously annotated translation of an Italian work portraying the romantic agony; a typescript paper on the Malcontent in the Jacobean Theatre. Do they know you are informing on them? They like to suppose so, they yearn to be taken seriously.

Do you expect a reward for this information? Not really.

In Singapore communists were a familiar occasion for cautions and constraints. I had not myself encountered a single one. (But remember the old joke: 'Are you a communist?' 'We're not allowed to say.') Until the evening when I entered the gents at a bar, and was accosted by a furious citizen, unknown to me, plainly a believer in that fallacious line of reasoning, one's enemy's enemy is one's friend. 'You have let us down!' he spluttered. 'You should have kept up the fight!' But how, exactly? He paused to check on his zip, and made for the door. 'You should have resigned your position and gone home.' So that's what fighting means.

※※

DEATH announced of Ai Qing at the age of 86. The obituarist—an author's last reviewer—remarks somewhat oddly that had he been lucky enough to die as early as certain distinguished predecessors, his reputation might have stood higher. What is meant is that he had to stand the full brunt of communism during its most rabid period, and hence was obliged 'to do much unsavoury tub-thumping in print'. Not to be born is best?

One good point is made. Ai Qing was born into a relatively prosperous family, but a fortune teller declared that he would inflict harm on his parents and consequently he was sent away to be nursed by a poor peasant woman. This alone could have driven him into the rational arms of communism, that enemy of ancient superstitions, though no doubt there were other reasons. Cast into prison by the Kuomintang in 1932, soon after he had joined the League of Leftwing Artists, he wrote his most famous poem:

> 'I am the son of a landlord,
> But I have been brought up on Dayanhe's milk:
> The son of Dayanhe . . .
> Dayanhe, today your foster-child is in jail,
> Writing a poem of praise, dedicated to you,
> Dedicated to your spirit, purple shade under the brown soil,
> Dedicated to your outstretched arms that embraced me, . . .
> Dedicated to your breasts that suckled me,
> Dedicated to your sons, my brothers,
> Dedicated to all of them on earth,
> The wet-nurses like my Dayanhe, and all their sons.'
>
> (translated by Eugene Chen Eoyang)

In the preface to his *Selected Poems* (Beijing, 1982) Ai Qing relates impassively, 'In April 1958, with the help of a general and the consent of Premier Zhou Enlai, I went to a state farm in the north-east to "observe and learn from real life".' Then in the winter of 1959 'I went to Xinjiang where I spent sixteen years in a reclamation area with a production and construction corps. I made many friends there.' In the Chronology an item (which must have crept in unnoticed) tells us: '1967: He is sent to a "farm" for "work rectification". He sleeps in a cellar; he is assigned to the latrine detail.'

'May you live in interesting times' is said to be an old Chinese curse. It would be misguided in us to envy Ai Qing his interesting subject-matter; it is worse than misguided to scold him for failing to invite a bullet in the back of his neck.

The last poem in this volume is 'Hong Kong', dated 1980/81, which begins with the poet (rehabilitated and allowed to travel) prudently aghast at this 'strange, uncanny city', 'with "freedom" as the siren song', its 'avarice and rapacity', double-decker buses and unnerving police cars, its night-life ('music and dance/Full of luxury and lust'), and lavish feasts laid out in the midst of poverty. And yet he wants to praise it, for millions of his compatriots have worked and struggled here, and moreover it is 'the conduit in and out of the motherland', 'the market-place for the exchange of goods', 'the bridge that leads to the four seas, the five continents', a creator of 'incalculable wealth and riches'. Which is exactly what Hong Kong's businessmen hope and trust it will continue to be under the new dispensation. Some other residents worry about that fading siren song.

The caring reader cares for what he reads.
    First 200 pages: people starve, are imprisoned, raped, shelled, beheaded, sell their daughters. Second 200 pages: people are tortured, shot, garrotted, torn to pieces by dogs, and save themselves by denouncing other people. Third 200 pages: people are purged, beaten, burnt to death, hang themselves, inform on their neighbours, kill babies and eat them.
    The pages turn more and more rapidly, the bookmark leaps ahead. The caring reader takes care of himself.
    The book becomes a bestseller.

No, I didn't want to climb yet another hill, to trudge round yet another temple. I was tired. And the temple probably looked better from a distance, as do the spectral lines of Mount Fuji, cleansed of human detritus.
    Our guides, men of letters, were much put out. Arrangements had been arranged. If one little thing went slightly wrong, who knows what big things might go very wrong? I would be quite happy left on my own for a while, I murmured. But as the rest of the party trooped away, one guide—no word spoken—remained at my elbow.
    Oh dear, perhaps he had wished to pace piously round this piece of Chinese history. Had I hurt his patriotic feelings? Or could he too be secretly glad of a rest? Impossible to tell. He was—a racial trait, or peculiar to writers?—inscrutable.

At least I refrained from mentioning foreign Fuji and distance lending enchantment. He pulled out a battered cigarette. I pulled out my pipe. To modify William Empson's words, provoked by an incipient earthquake: The guarded tourist makes the guardian guide the test.

February 1998: 'Chinese send four poets to prison.' The poets are accused of proposing to publish a new poetry magazine, advocating a 'literary renaissance', without official permission, and of conducting 'poetry salons'. Guilty, you could say, of a gross breach of inscrutability.

That exquisite sense of courtesy. What one best—in a sense, worst, most woeful—remembers of certain countries one has passed through. How, without resenting what you say or the fact that you are free to say it, they strive, without betraying embarrassment, to find a noncommittal or oblique response, one which makes some sense but not an unfortunate one, which won't in the least hurt your feelings and won't (they hope) turn out to hurt them.

※

HERE is Nietzsche (virtually the only modern philosopher who seems to mean something, whether or no you care for what he seems to mean) on the subject of Schopenhauer (possibly the one other modern philosopher who seems to mean something):
    Schopenhauer, the true educator, the philosopher whom Nietzsche anticipated in his callow youth, one 'whom one could follow without any misgiving because one would have more faith in him than one had in oneself', the taskmaster through whom we become '*able* to educate ourselves *against* our age'.

'We feel that here we shall always find a bracing air.' For Schopenhauer has 'a cheerfulness that really cheers'. A cheerfulness that cheers Nietzsche, that is; for, as he says, there are two quite different kinds of cheerfulness, Schopenhauer's belonging to the harsher. (Cf. Thomas Mann on Schopenhauer's 'fierce and caustic mockery of life' which nevertheless 'fills the reader with strange, deep satisfaction'.) In portraying the solitaries, 'free in spirit', 'encompassed by a net of misunderstandings', brimming with 'volcanic menace', who emerge from their inward caves 'wearing a terrifying aspect', whose words and deeds are explosions (and who may conceivably perish by their own hand), Nietzsche is talking about himself.

If not himself as he was, then as he wished he were or thought he had to be, himself as 'his first sacrifice to himself'. In fact there is little here about Schopenhauer's thinking. The essay turns into an assault on universities as an arm of the state and on academic philosophers, 'this officially recognized guild of pseudo-thinkers'. The epitaph of university philosophy ought to be: 'It disturbed nobody.' (*Untimely Meditations*, translated by R. J. Hollingdale.)

Nietzsche on the universities: 'Linguistic studies, for example, are pursued more zealously than ever, but no one considers it necessary to educate himself in correct writing and speaking.' In his 'caustic mockery', his fierce pursuit of what matters (for good or for ill), he reminds one of Leavis.

Philosophers, even (or especially) the more meaningful, can get things wrong. On the subject of convention-bound societies, Nietzsche quotes an Englishman as saying that 'A Shelley would not have been able to live in England, and a race of Shelleys would have been impossible.' (Just as well, that last bit.) The Englishman was Walter Bagehot, in *Physics and Politics*, speaking of New England.

On translation, Nietzsche appears to have been of the same opinion as George Steiner. What is least successfully carried over from one language to another, he wrote in *Beyond Good and Evil*, is the tempo of its style, 'which has its origin in the character of the race, or, expressed more physiologically, in the average tempo of its "metabolism"'. His real quarry is the German language. 'The German is virtually incapable of *presto* in his language', and hence 'of many of the most daring and delightful nuances of free, free-spirited thought'. 'Everything staid, sluggish, ponderously solemn, all long-winded and boring species of style have been developed in profuse multiplicity among the Germans.' Who would venture on a German rendering of Machiavelli (with his 'boisterous *allegrissimo*'), or Petronius ('a master of *presto* in invention, ideas, words'), let alone Aristophanes? Whereas how well Nietzsche goes into English!

It must be by a lapse of taste or remarkable hardihood that the Goethe Institute in London announces a season of German comedy films of the 1990s under the rubric, 'We Have Ways of Making You Laugh'. The leaflet begins by asking, 'Is German humour a contradiction in terms?' Well, there is humour of one sort or another in virtually all the major German writers from Goethe—oh yes—to Thomas Mann and beyond. But major writers of any nation are exceptions rather than exemplars. 'A German comedy,' said George Eliot, an admirer of other products of the national mind, 'is like a German sentence: you see no reason in its structure why it should ever come to an end, and you accept the conclusion as an arrangement of Providence rather than of the author.'

The films to be shown at the Goethe Institute don't promise a load of laughs. One is 'a shamelessly old-fashioned fairy tale, glamorously set in Berlin and New York and featuring a mouth-watering array of fabulous Austrian food'. In another, juxtaposing the former West Germany and the former East Germany, 'what began as a Walter Mitty episode threatens to become a fully-fledged political scandal'. The leading actor in a third is (ingratiatingly?) described as 'a kind of German Ernie Wise with occasional Cleesian overtones'. Then there's a short in which Erich Honecker, former head of state of East Germany, confesses to Pope John Paul II, and another, *Der schönste Busen der Welt*, where 'a voluptuous secretary bumps into a sexist businessman' and 'the eponymous breasts are mysteriously transferred to him'.

However, a German director explains all: 'Film-goers used to wallow masochistically in heavy art-house movies. Today they are falling over themselves laughing at daft comedies.' They have found ways of making themselves laugh. Good luck to them.

And then came the *Frankfurter Allgemeine Zeitung* and its reference to our government minister as 'the Jew Rifkind'. Taxed with this quaint identification, the youthful journalist declared herself amazed to gather that the word 'Jew' was considered offensive in Britain. She used it only because she thought it surprising that a Jew should quote Luther. But what's so surprising about that? Mr Rifkind was *Foreign* Secretary. And Luther was forever quoting Jews. He translated some of them.

OPIUM, De Quincey noted, has a powerful effect on the sense of space. In his dreams, 'buildings, landscapes, &c. were exhibited in proportions so vast as the bodily eye is not fitted to receive. Space swelled, and was amplified to an extent of unutterable infinity.'

In the only dream of this kind I recall—it would be forty years back—I was approaching the Hongkong & Shanghai Bank in Bangkok, a solid respectable building, as banks used to be before they went in for black glass and chromium. As I drew level, the bank grew an extra dimension or two, opening out into ranks of turrets, corridors or colonnades, and courtyards within courtyards, as suddenly as if it were some glorified pop-up book, luminous and above all spacious.

Around the same time my wife dreamt that she had found a cat, squashed flat, outside the house. She picked up the two-dimensional corpse and made to drop it into the dustbin. Whereupon it began to swell out, rapidly, like a balloon being pumped up, into a super-cat of architectonic proportions.

Neither dream is up to De Quincey's splendours; nor down to his Asiatic horrors, as when he came on Isis and Osiris, who told him he had done a deed at which the ibis and the crocodile trembled, but which didn't deter the latter from pressing 'cancerous kisses' on him. De Quincey had some bad trips. But he was drinking huge doses in the form of laudanum, more potent than opium as smoked. And, as he said, 'the varieties of effect produced by opium on different constitutions are infinite'. What you get depends on what you bring.

'Dreams become a wonderful study: the various ingenuities of their unpleasantness.' Thus Ruskin, who records in his *Diaries* an example of the type of dream, not uncommon, that sets out masterfully, all confidence, and then declines into humiliating farce. (The unconscious, at times disconcertingly conscious, has its Mephistophelean moods.) He was arguing against others that a certain picture was a Mantegna, and declared that the picture was recognized as such in Italy, where its beautiful representation of Christ had inspired 'ever so many' novels. Someone present couldn't understand how a religious picture would make people write novels. So Ruskin sat down to read an extract from one of those novels, and show how good they were. Having accidentally turned over two pages together, before he was aware, he was reading out a passage describing 'all sorts of things that were not proper to be described'. He was interrupted by someone, seemingly his mother, sitting down to play the piano. (Which his mother never did.) The others present in the dream observed that the interruption came most opportunely.

A Grub Street dream. Am at some sort of literary party. A crowd of people are moving along a high gallery, purposefully, though the purpose escapes me; perhaps in search of a drink. I ask a young woman—after some hesitation while trying to remember whether his name rhymes with finder or tinder—if a certain person is still literary editor of a certain paper. (I think uneasily of soliciting some reviewing from him.) Yes, she says, he is still there, but about to move to the Greyhound. Going to the dogs, eh? The witticism, which pleases me immensely, is received with a grudging sniff. To redeem myself: But what is the Greyhound? An archive, she explains, to do with presidents and vice-presidents of the United States. I wake up, feeling foolish and uncouth.

Lao-tzu has something to the effect that he who feels punctured must have been a bubble. Interpretation unnecessary. Embarrassment caused me to make twenty mistakes in typing the dream out.

A typical author's dream, I imagine. You have submitted a typescript to a publisher, and heard nothing for several weeks. Then the mail van delivers a huge parcel, in shape like a rolled-up carpet. You can barely open it. It has been out in the rain; also it appears to have been treated with tar. The outer wrappings, when at last you remove them, carry away part of the contents. Which must include an enormous report on your typescript. What little you can decipher, smudged, torn, in places reversed out, white lettering on black, seems to bear no relation to you or yours. Or is peculiarly oblique in style. You would read between the lines if you could read the lines. Eventually you wake up, your fingers sticky with tar, or sweat.

Coleridge wrote that dreams were sometimes useful in giving the feelings of visual sense to 'the well-grounded fears and hopes of the understanding'. Useful?

A characteristic dream of old age. Getting hopelessly lost in a strange city, of dark streets and desolate underpasses, where an unrecognizable language is spoken. You are grilled by a policeman, whom you understand only too well, from whom you escape, to be lost again. You think of phoning home, but you don't have the foreign money, or you can't find a slot to put coins in, or else you have forgotten your number (you have the numbers in your head, but not the order).

When at last you wake, even your bed seems not your own. If only interpretation were called for.

(When Ann Faraday, a dream researcher, dreamt about a fish entering her ear, her analyst interpreted it as a wish for sexual intercourse. She had been thinking of the play *Hamlet*, and her own feeling, which the analyst declined to consider, was that she was being poisoned by his interpretations, which she received through her ear.)

Scrappy hospital dreams these nights. Unable to locate the right ward in a huge building shaped like a battleship: will be late for appointment . . . Getting ratty when told I must wait another seven hours to see the consultant: 'And he'll want you to come back tomorrow' . . . Going up and down in vast primitive lifts, open on all sides, looking for a lavatory; many doors invite, but open on distressful scenes, anything but what's wanted . . . Lifting shirt to reveal evidence of gynaecomastia; the surgeon gasps: 'Both of them!' Tiresias at last.

(Waking life. You come from under the drear skies of Tooting into a hospital ward all too well lighted, without a saving shadow. Regions of sorrow, marks of weakness, marks of woe. The poets have been here long before you. Do they help? They certainly heighten. In fact there's an air of cool normality, and a surprising incidence of cheerfulness, almost *joie de vivre*, you tell yourself, crossing your fingers. You won't miss those gloomy, littered streets too much.)

Walter Benjamin warns: 'The narration of dreams brings calamity, because a person still half in league with the dream world betrays it in his words and must incur its revenge.' This doesn't inhibit Benjamin from narrating a dream of his own, from which he awoke laughing at a learned polyglot pun.

SCHOPENHAUER notes that while a woman surprised in the act of generation (i.e. of sex) would wish to sink into the depths of the earth, she will carry her pregnancy without a trace of shame, even with pride. Yet the pregnancy is the sign and sequel of the sexual act. This 'significant phenomenon' he ascribes to the fact that pregnancy in a certain sense brings with it a purgation of the guilt attaching to the coitus. The latter is chiefly the man's affair, whereas the pregnancy is wholly the woman's.

Apropos of the old Christian view that coitus is permissible only for the sake of procreation, Schopenhauer then asserts that bringing a child into the world deliberately, cold-bloodedly, in the absence of any 'subjective passion', love or lust or whatever, is a highly questionable moral action. It stands in the same relation to generation from mere or sheer sexual impulse as does a cold-blooded, deliberate murder to an unpremeditatedly fatal stroke delivered in anger. (A distinction currently much exercised in cases of abused wives killing brutal husbands.)

What would Schopenhauer have to say about artificial insemination? The woman will still be proud to exhibit her pregnancy, despite there being no guilt to purge away. The man's feelings are rarely dwelt on, but judging by television appearances we may assume that he has no pressing wish to sink into the depths of the earth.

Schopenhauer was averse to beards, as comprising a kind of partial mask, and believed they ought to be legally prohibited. Also because a beard is an indication of sex standing in the very forefront of the face, and hence obscene—which is why beards please women. Is he making a joke? It's hard to tell what is going on when philosophers let their hair down and engage in the playful speculations of common humanity.

A philosopher has recently summed it up: philosophy is an activity *sui generis*, it does not consist in knowing and is not inspired by truth. (So it must bear much the same relationship to life as modern literary theory does to literature.)

In his book *Quiddities*, W. V. Quine sets out to define *Knowledge* but gives the notion up as 'a bad job', referring us to epistemology, which is the theory of—er—knowledge. *Truth* isn't too good a job, either. 'The sentence "Snow is white" is true if and only if it is a fact that snow is white', and 'to attribute truth to the sentence is to attribute whiteness to the snow'; which cancels the quotation marks: 'truth is disquotation'. I can't follow what is happening here, but apparently it is just as well that truth cannot be defined, since its 'genuine definability' would be 'lethal'. Lethal to truth? To Pilate? To all of us? The truth shall make us free, someone else claimed; truth has always had a mixed press.

However, Quine describes his book as 'an intermittently philosophical dictionary'—human kind cannot bear very much philosophy—and so understanding may await us elsewhere, and even knowledge, even truth.

Although Quine finds himself loath to kick a concept when it is down, *Belief* comes in for quite a buffeting. More attractively, belief is a disposition, whereas thinking is an activity, even if sedentary: 'We sit and think, but do we sit and believe?' (We are supposed to stand up for our beliefs.) He wonders whether Keats really believed that 'Beauty is truth, truth beauty', or whether he was 'merely bent on creating a bit of beauty on his own'. (Incidentally, the sequential 'that is all ye need to know' should lift a considerable burden from our schoolteachers.) People will go to any lengths for a rhyme; Quine cites a pleasing instance: 'Fair Naples sleeping, a vigil keeping'. The dictionary tells us that 'vigil' means 'keeping awake during the time usually given to sleep', but it's easy to get hold of the wrong end of the stick.

Communication: Quine observes that two things are commonly said to be communicated, diseases and ideas. In 1987 he wasn't speaking of the Internet; no news is good news. *Euphemisms*: 'My God!' was softened, deblasphemized, into (foreign languages don't count) 'Dio mio!', and thence into 'dear me', harmless if a shade narcissistic. My mother used to euphemize 'devil'—as in 'What/Who the devil'—into 'divil', uttered with such unwonted fierceness that for me it came to portend some fate worse than Satan. The word 'Chinaman', Quine contends, was actually a painstaking distortion of the normal English linguistic pattern with the polite aim of conforming to the Chinese expression, 'djung-kuo run', 'China man': well-meaning, but usage has made it, as dictionaries say, *derog.* and hence *offens.* (When the young man later known as Sax Rohmer asked the ouija board how he could make a good living, the answer came: 'C-H-I-N-A-M-A-N'; and Fu Manchu was born.) The word survives, presumably causing no offence, as a term in cricket for a left-handed bowler's offbreak to a right-handed batsman.

Quine has an amusing passage on advertising. Some large soup cans—large because the soup is not concentrated—bear the legend, 'Full strength; no need to add water'. And there's a canner of salmon whose product was, for some reason not divulged, persistently white. He made 'a spurious virtue of this chromatic deficiency' by declaring on the label: 'Guaranteed not to turn red in the can'. On words Quine is great. (Except when attempting to subsume 'mind' into 'body', and even then he disarms: 'I have been accused of denying consciousness, but I am not conscious of having done so.') It was for the sake of 'semi-illiterate tailgaters' who might muddle the two senses of the prefix 'in' (e.g., 'innocuous' = not nocuous whereas 'invaluable' = very valuable indeed), that the warning on the back of petrol tankers was changed to 'flammable'. Even semi-illiterates, Quine allows, shouldn't be burnt for their heresies.

Then there is the growing popularity of the slash or oblique stroke, '/', which typographers with some grasp of history call a 'solidus'. Not because the slash is notably solid, but because the Latin *solidus* was a Roman coin, roughly equated with our erstwhile shilling, and the slash, a deformation of the long 's', was the sign denoting shilling. And from *solidus* came 'soldat', 'soldier' (he took the King's shilling), and (but oh how fallen!) the 'sou'. Housman's army of mercenaries may have saved the sum of things for sous.

In a light-hearted, serious-minded essay on punctuation, Theodor Adorno likens the exclamation mark to an index finger raised in warning and the question mark to a flashing light or the blink of an eye.

The ellipsis, . . . , suggests an infinitude of thoughts and associations, 'something the hack journalist does not have', but is happy to simulate. (Once upon a time these dots stood in for thoughts and associations which it would be imprudent to spell out; this consideration no longer obtains.) 'A colon, says Karl Kraus, opens its mouth wide: woe to the writer who does not fill it with something nourishing'; and the semicolon, Adorno reckons, resembles a drooping moustache ('I am even more aware of its gamy taste'). You may omit punctuation marks as superfluous, but they are still there, in hiding, 'friendly spirits whose bodiless presence nourishes the body of language'.

Exclamation marks have become intolerable, though, 'usurpers of authority, assertions of importance'. German expressionism deployed them 'to vouch for its effect, and it went up in smoke along with them'; seen in such texts today 'they look like the multiple zeros on the banknotes printed during the German inflation'. (Even so, they have their uses on occasion!) As for the dash, this makes thought become aware of its fragmentary character, Adorno contends, which is why dilettantes like to hook sentences and phrases together in the hope of suggesting a logical relationship which isn't there. So, in our linguistically degenerate age, all that this dangerously revealing sign is allowed to do is 'prepare us in a foolish way for surprises that by that very token are no longer surprising'. When dashes work in pairs it is different. The cautious writer will prefer to place parenthetical matter between dashes rather than within brackets, for brackets remove that matter from the sentence, relegating it as superfluous (see the parenthesis, 'Once upon a time . . .', above), whereas in good prose nothing should be unnecessary to the whole.

Quotation marks are to be employed only when quoting, and should be rejected as an ironic device, for the sound reason that 'they violate the very concept of irony by separating it from the matter at hand and presenting a predetermined judgement on the subject'. But what to do in a time averse to irony and unwilling to make an effort to recognize it? The ironist wouldn't want us to suppose he really meant what he said. And the 'petit signe flagellateur', a reversed question mark proposed in 1899, though apt, would be no better: another flashing light, 'On guard, irony ahead!' The ironist will need to be clever. (Which is what he is supposed to be—and often disliked for being.)

Of German quotation marks—» «—Adorno observes that they lick their lips 'with self-satisfied peasant cunning'. (Cunning it may be, but not wholly self-satisfying, to quote somebody else's words when you know you can't improve on them.) Or they might be thought to be trumpeting something of real or factitious moment. In which case it follows that French quotation marks—« »—must be doing the opposite, like sharp-eyed brackets, pointing backwards to what has gone before and forwards to what is coming after, referring us to the main, more important text. Our simple-minded British signs merely betoken the arrival of another voice and then its departure.

Punctuation lands us in a permanent predicament which, were we fully aware of it while writing, would oblige us 'to give up writing altogether'. (That would be the day, exclamation mark.) The writer cannot trust in the rules, which are often rigid and crude; nor can he safely ignore them. He must be guided by 'a tactful sensitivity'. (Something which, I take it, operates in the choice of words and throughout the process of writing.) You only break the rule when you become conscious of a new one, one that obtains, perhaps uniquely, at that one moment, in that one place. Adorno grows almost mystical: 'In every punctuation mark thoughtfully avoided, writing pays homage to the sound it suppresses.' Or: ('something nourishing' coming up) since he compares punctuation marks with cadences in music, you play by ear, and hope you have a good one.

Talking of irony . . . ('an infinitude of thoughts and associations') . . . Irony tends to attract ironies. It having been decided to use Louis Boilly's 'Les Grimaces' as cover picture for a book on irony, the publisher asks Göttingen University's Art Collection to provide a colour transparency. This arrives, the envelope is opened, and the contents fall straight into the mouth of a puppy who happens to be in the office, and are swallowed. (In what spirit is not known.) The puppy suffers no ill effects. Unlike the transparency.

❧

STURDILY independent, and quite right too. We are not going to let those European Courts boss us about! Except when we lose our case at home. Then we run to the European Court of Human Rights.

We are not going to print those deplorable photographs any more. We print them to show the kind of thing we are not going to print any more. We are very much against this shameful book. We print extracts from it to show why.

You dislike 'the times'. But you have to keep up with them, you mustn't get left behind. By keeping up with 'the times' you make them fractionally worse. But you don't dislike them quite so much now.

During the first assembly of the year, the headmistress of a private primary school concludes her address to the new pupils: 'So, if you have a problem, you know where to go for help, don't you?' A girl of five or six pipes up: 'Yes, the bank!' Worldly wisdom out of the mouth of an infant. Those proposing to teach morality should take note of what they are up against.

Family values, sliding scale . . . Bring back flogging! Bring back transportation! Bring back hanging! Oh very well, but at least bring back marriage.

Have come across a book on moral problems—more exactly the problem of morals—which proves to be purely philosophical, theoretical, and doesn't invoke a single example, not one moral problem you or I might encounter. The book may not thrill, but it makes for easeful reading.

'A moral philosophy should be inhabited,' writes Iris Murdoch, after quoting Kierkegaard's description of the Hegelian system as a grand palace set up by someone who then lived in a hovel.

'We should feel like savages if we had to believe in morality,' C. H. Sisson observes sadly.

'A man, to be greatly good, must imagine intensely and comprehensively; he must put himself in the place of another and of many others; the pains and pleasures of his species must become his own. The great instrument of moral good is the imagination.'

The word 'morality' was never once spoken in the family, it being the perquisite of a different class of beings, and smacking of hypocrisy, affectation, privilege, tendentious repression. ('Behold the moral Pecksniff! . . . a direction-post which is always telling the way to a place, and never goes there.') In adolescence I cherished Shelley's *Defence of Poetry*, even preferring it to his poetry. (As I still do, despite some loss of idealism incurred through the years.) Morality *there* was a completely different matter!

I had Shelley's essay in *The Prelude to Poetry*, an excellent compilation published in Everyman's Library in 1927. There was a curious sentence in the text: 'Every epoch, under names more or less specious, has defied its peculiar errors.' I am gratified to see my correction in the margin: 'deified'.

WE are born makers-of-sense, whatever sense can be made; we are drawn to track down the whys and wherefores. The urge, or need, seems to grow stronger with the years. Hence the appeal of detective stories. Ignorance, uncertainty, confusion, suspicion, false leads—then the tying up of loose ends, and the making of sense. A trivial pursuit for books, those sacred objects, to engage in? But books engage in many pursuits, some of them worse. There is a time for the detective story; which, since in age we tend to have time, needn't interfere with reading or rereading Proust, Musil, Mann, Dickens . . . Even making sense of things that possess little sense brings some relief. There's no call to be ashamed of that, is there?

Remember the doctor, working in a refugee camp, children dying around him, whatever was happening they were innocent of it—the doctor who, when at last he slumped into bed, reached for a Sherlock Holmes story. A mystery satisfactorily solved, it helped him to sleep.

Here today, gone tomorrow. Certainly no theme for a serious writer. So you detach yourself from the ephemeral. Where does that leave you? Free to embrace the eternal verities? Perhaps so, and your verses or whatever will endure for ever. But why does the ephemeral tug at you so insistently? Because you live in it, it's what you truly know? So many questions! Then the eternal verities, flaunting their prestige, do their utmost to entice you back. Is time on their side? Whose side is time on? Two voices calling—can you honestly distinguish one from the other?

No sooner said than a poem by Piotr Sommer arrives from Warsaw. Certain writers, it remarks, are waiting till readers and editors tire, as they must, of 'this infantile disease/of civic-mindedness/or whatever you call it', and finally turn to them:

> And we'll open our drawers
> and take out our Timeless Values
> which, precisely because they're timeless,
> can now
> wait calmly.

Princess Diana and the Matter of Britain. We desire, maybe need, an occasional orgy of communal emotion, above all of grief, perhaps (strictly speaking) inordinate: the peculiar satisfaction of sharing for a while in the collective mind or heart. Or, since cynicism isn't invariably in place, what happens at such times can be an upsurge of the goodness that people customarily suppress in themselves out of embarrassment.

And then, an indistinct but obdurate sense of the mythical—a habit carried in our bones—attaches to the Princess's life and death. A myth, in its fullness no simple, unalloyed one, I wouldn't care to expound. (That some have judged her 'self-indulgent', 'a seriously disturbed young woman', is beside the point. The same could be said of Artemis, an avid hunter of stags, quick to take offence and to get her own back on the offender.) A particular presence is signalled by her name, which in his funeral tribute her brother noted as an 'irony'. And which is similarly manifest in a poem written by Andrew Motion. 'Your life was not your own to keep/or lose': virtually a definition of the protagonist of myth. He invokes and inverts the legend: 'Diana, breathless, hunted by your own quick hounds'. Perhaps 'quick hounds' —paparazzi as euphemistic Eumenides—is too specific for myth, or simply incongruous. But the poem had to come to a prompt end, not so much rounded off as reined in. And ellipsis wouldn't have been seemly . . .

Yet we don't altogether *like* myths, grizzled despots out of the barbaric past, throwing their bogus weight about. We would rather work things out for ourselves. But working things out can be quite tiring.

'"The horror of that moment," the King went on, "I shall never, *never* forget!"'

"You will, though," the Queen said, "if you don't make a memorandum of it."' (*Through the Looking-Glass*.)

❧

OLD people on trial. Alan Bennett notes that a zimmer frame is a sort of portable dock. Wherever you go, you bump into judge and jury.

Far too many of us, a drain on the economy. (Cf. captains of commerce, who earn so much that they must be Stakhanovites as well as geniuses. They'll never be a burden, aside from those who have to be accommodated at the public expense; they'll never be 'old people'.) What to do with us? Abandon us on some high, inhospitable mountain? Only if we can afford the taxi fare.

An ecclesiastical dignitary once came up with a splendid proposal for putting unwanted Irish babies to good use. We oldies are too tough, in one sense, for that solution. Still, even horses' hooves have proved serviceable.

(When offered any marmalade other than Frank Cooper's Oxford, Leavis would wave it away: 'Horses' hooves, horses' hooves!')

There's an ill-concealed hatred of the *old*. My wife's car having suffered superficial damage, the repairers proposed to write it off: it was eight years old. That my wife was attached to it struck them as a sign of shared senility. And when our fridge fell silent, the engineer who came to look at it advised us to throw it out and buy a new one forthwith. To show his contempt, he turned the fridge upside down and shook it; whereupon it began to hum. It worked perfectly for the next three years. A warning: Don't turn old people upside down and shake them.

Age brings an attachment to age, in clothes for instance. A pair of trousers which lost all semblance of a crease years ago, and here and there hint at the flesh beneath. Sandals which are paper-thin, held together by invisible threads. I am given a new pair, handsome, shining with youth, the right size—except they don't seem quite to fit my feet.

When someone gave him a new mountain shawl, Amiel said of his old one that it reminded him of the centaur's tunic which couldn't be torn off without carrying away the flesh and blood of its wearer.

Capsules for incipient ulcer. Impossible to open the damned container. Is one *that* feeble? 'Created sick, commanded to be sound.' Incipient ulcer grows more incipient.

'How To Open': the incomprehensible diagram on the cap resembles the stylized matchstick figures in an illustrated edition of the *Kama Sutra* that once came my way.

This seems odd, considering what care for our well-being, what awareness of our stupidity, manufacturers so often show. A pack of sleeping-pills carries the warning, 'May cause drowsiness'; on a packet of peanuts, 'Contains nuts'; attached to a common domestic appliance, 'Do not iron clothes on body'.

At the vet's. The patients are on their best behaviour. Not a squeak out of them. Birds wouldn't melt in the cats' mouths. The dogs never chased a cat in their lives. Then a kitten mews. They all look faintly shocked.

At the doctor's. The patients are on their best behaviour. Not a sigh out of them. They never told fibs. They wouldn't get drunk or chase the opposite sex. Then a baby hiccups. They all look faintly shocked.

Am proof-reading an expanded Collected Poems—fifty years of them. In the early ones, so many words at whose meaning I have to guess, words I've never used since. Rather wish I had, some of them sound quite impressive. Reminds me of a catch-phrase current when I was a kid: 'Must have swallowed a dictionary.'

And some of the poems I just can't understand now; obscure, so they ought to be good. Unless I've grown peculiarly dim.

Rather depressing. I can believe what they say about thousands of brain cells dying every day. Like words fading out of the dictionaries one once swallowed.

Looking for one's pipe, then realizing it's in one's mouth, or for one's specs, pushed back on top of one's head. That can happen to anyone. But again and again—looking up foreign words in bilingual dictionaries, English/French, English/German, in the wrong half of the book. What is nature trying to tell me? That English is the official language of the afterworld, and not to bother with other tongues? ('English is the language that opens every door,' R. S. Thomas has said plaintively. 'It will be the same in heaven. After reaching the gates and asking Saint Peter in Welsh, "May I come in?", the answer will be, "Speak English, man."')

What is distinctly worse, I tell myself *dictionary*, I must look up some word in the *dictionary*, to check on spelling or pronunciation. When I arrive at the word, I gaze at it uncomprehendingly: it is 'dictionary'.

The joke quoted by Freud—'Experience consists in experiencing what we do not wish to experience'—has ceased to be a joke. How could one ever have smiled over it? Yet—the thought crosses one's mind, at some speed—it is better to experience something than not to experience at all.

Now M. de Charlus was a proud man. After a stroke, he found himself uttering one word or phrase in mistake for another. He would then check swiftly on the words he had started out with and, showing infinite ingenuity, so construct the rest of the sentence that it followed naturally from the initial error—which now, by this contrivance, appeared to have been intended. He must have had his wits about him.

Charlus as a 'role model'!

※

SUNDRY embarrassments.

'The contents of this envelope are important and require your immediate attention.' To begin with, opening the envelope is a major undertaking, and wouldn't be easy if you were in full possession of your fingers. And then, though you labour to make them so, the contents are not in the least important to you, nor you to them. Why is everything *important* these days? Because so many things are of no consequence.

A young fellow is skating at speed along the pavement. As I cringe back against the wall to let him pass unhindered, I see he is speaking importantly into a mobile phone.

How advanced everything is! Mind you, this week's horoscope says that mine is the most spiritually advanced of all signs. Also that the current aspect of Jupiter and Saturn will ensure that I get what I deserve—and if I don't like what I get I must be honest and blame myself. So honesty and blaming oneself is what being spiritually advanced amounts to. I feel myself cringing against a wall.

My wife dreams we are both diagnosed as suffering from Creutzfeldt-Jakob disease; rather than repining, she tries in the dream to remember when we last ate beef. During the same night I dream that a doctor, wielding a scalpel or possibly a spatula, informs me that I have AIDS. This doesn't worry me at all.

Are these dreams a complacent hypochondria, or a Shelleyan gesture towards human solidarity? Or merely the process likened by experts to an office shredder mincing up waste experiences or a computer-clearing mechanism?

'Dreams go by contraries': so said the experts some six centuries back. Then here's two diseases we don't have to worry about! But we weren't.

The phone rings inopportunely, and I stagger to it like a shackled prisoner. (There's something to be said for mobile phones.) A female voice asks for Denise. Perhaps the caller is French, they tend to pronounce my name that way. Does she want a girl, a lady, I ask. Two politically incorrect strikes against me. Unlike some miscallers, she remains composed and simply says Yes. So that's that. I stagger back to unfinished business.

Curious how some people who misdial get so ratty. The girl/woman or boy/man they desire has to be at this number, you are concealing that person's presence, you are a jealous or interloping lover or a hostile parent. Some years back we used to get urgent requests for Fifi, Lulu and the like. And also for a highly esteemed baby-sitter bearing our name. When we professed ignorance or innocence we stood accused of being or pretending to be neither a pimp nor a childcare agency.

Infuriating to hear the passenger-friendly announcer at Earl's Court assuring you that 'The train approaching is your Ealing Broadway train' or 'your Richmond train'. Or even 'your Wimbledon train', the one you have been waiting for. As if you are responsible for any shortcomings.

Cf. an impertinent contraption come across in some pubs: 'This is your FIRKIN NUT MACHINE 1 × 20p'.

Cf. 'This was your life', 'These are your pains', 'This is your death approaching'.

Modesty: the Cinderella of the virtues, the poor relative, even—there's something obnoxious about its bleating—the black sheep of the holy family. At best an admission of mediocrity. If you make claims for yourself, in a friendly spirit others will knock fifty per cent off; if you don't make claims, what will they, in exasperation, knock the fifty per cent off?

What a nice mind your fingers have! You wanted to write 'virago' and it came out 'virgin'. (This week your horoscope says, 'You're too nice for your own good.' How nice.)

'. . . but is it art?' That's not the right question. (It may be begging one.) The right question is: but is it true? (And that, someone's bound to object, is begging the question.)

Incredible, the games that words get up to, seemingly without our playing any part, in our very absence. A story that sticks in my mind was told by a master at Warwick School whom I knew in my youth. In a record shop he had asked for *Songs on the Death of Children*. The young assistant searched for a while, then informed him, 'I'm afraid we don't seem to have anything by that title exactly, but perhaps this would do?', handing him *Pavane for a Dead Infanta*.

Have frequently been admonished for committing excruciating puns, a sort of offence against the literary person. (Condoning would be a fitter word; they came to me, I didn't go to them.) For example— here the rebuke came from an authority on German literature whom I admired—when Faust's mistress, Helen (formerly of Troy), had disappeared, and Mephistopheles insinuated, 'Gone to Paris for the weekend.'

Have learnt my lesson, I think. Please note that on pp. 153–4, in connection with the parable of the fig tree, not once is the word 'figurative' to be seen.

What did you say?

Because of the poets, because of the newspapers,
because of . . . we have turned to *Sprachkritik*,
the which puts paid to the pretensions of words
and their (as once one deemed them) meanings.
Indeed there are things we do not care to say
(not necessarily those that men of letters
sometimes make their livings out of), but this
is our cowardice or caution, not the falsity
or futility of words. We can't tell what they
mean? We tell from their context: other words.
Or would you rather I painted a picture?
Really I would say no more on this subject,
though not because words fail me. Rather,
it's we fail them. Selbstkritik is the word,
not in italics, it isn't meant to be foreign.

❦

ONE of Yasunari Kawabata's more meaningful 'palm-of-the-hand' stories concerns a village outside Kyoto, famous for cherry-blossom viewing, which had no public lavatory. An enterprising villager built a little privy, charging three coins for the use of it. Before long he was a rich man by local standards. Another villager then set up a rival establishment, in the shape of a formal tea-room, luxuriously appointed, with an eye to visitors participating in the three-hour tea ceremony. He proposed to charge eight coins. Unfortunately the visitors thought the structure too beautiful for their needs, and he faced ruin. One day, however, during his absence from the scene, his privy was mobbed by customers. His wife, delighted and incredulous, as she counted up the takings, reckoned that her husband must have attained to Buddhahood, and at the end of the day she bought wine to celebrate. Alas, he arrived home dead, on a litter. Early that morning he had paid three coins to use the other lavatory, and he sat there all day, clearing his throat noisily whenever a customer approached. The long hot day, spent in cramped amd noxious conditions, proved too much for him. Some of the more sophisticated residents of Kyoto surmised that he had truly become a Buddha of the Loo.

Though disrelished by foreigners, the *benjo*, Japanese privy, embracing both *daiben* and *shōben*, big *ben* and little *ben*, has acquired a mystique among the natives. When a leading newspaper invited an austere Japanese scholar of my acquaintance to contribute to a series on reading in diverse circumstances—in the saddle, in a fishing-boat, at a hot spring, while viewing cherry-blossom—he chose 'Reading in the Benjo'.

'At least the children are told how to hold their knives properly and get walloped if they call the lavatory the toilet.' This example from a novel of 1990 by Joanna Trollope, says R. W. Burchfield in the *New Fowler's Modern English Usage*, 'neatly introduces the sociological problem about what was once called the water closet'. He judges that *toilet* is the first choice of the majority of people in Britain, 'universal in working-class speech and upwards into the language of many white-collar speakers', while '*lavatory* (now fading) and *loo* (especially) are the favourites of the chattering classes'.

Americans make use of a number of euphemisms which strike us (though no mean euphemists ourselves) as odd: 'restroom' (who would go there to rest?), 'comfort station' (rather too grand; but 'a comfort serves in a whirlwind'), 'powder room' (sexist?), 'john' (who?), 'can' (ugh!). Not a patch on our 'khazi' (from the Arabic, no less).

In my childhood we called it 'lavatory'. (Well, 'lavertree', if you insist.) Not that we'd have got walloped if we said 'toilet'; we didn't get walloped for words, though 'loo' would have drawn a sharp look. I expect we had heard of 'toilet', but it wasn't our kind of word. (Did we say 'toilet paper'? Probably just 'paper'.) As for 'bathroom', obviously not; there wasn't a bath.

One review of the present book's predecessor described it as 'a book of bits and bobs for the most refined sort of lavatory'. (Bits and bobs? Doesn't sound exactly refined.) Another deemed it 'ideal bedside material'. One is grateful for small mercies.

Such is the voracity of collectors, you don't have to be especially famous to get requests for autographs. Most are couched in terms so general as to fit anyone who has ever published anything. 'Your writing has provided me with many hours of enjoyment.' Often plus a pious gesture: 'Literature, whether prose or poetry, does indeed affect the course of mankind.' This one, from Elkhorn, Wisconsin, reaches a novel and disconcerting conclusion: 'I hope you will continue to farewell with your career.'

'They'll review this one for sure!' he tells himself. They don't. He writes another. 'It'll be different, this one they *must* take note of.' They don't. Writers tend to write, and he writes another. 'Ah, this time . . .' He dies before the book appears. Some while later, a huge uncouth fellow, brandishing a sort of trident and swishing his tail, comes up to him. 'By the way,' he leers, 'they didn't bother with your last, either.'

❧

MODERN instances can throw light on old saws. 'The poor man's shilling is but a penny': poorer people lack cars and can't get to the supermarket; they have to buy at their little local shops, and pay more for everything.

These are known as 'convenience shops': a term that evokes a picture of the carriage trade needing some common article in a hurry, and dispatching a footman for it.

One quality of a virtuous housewife, as set out in Proverbs: 'She is like the merchants' ships; she bringeth her food from afar.'

As necessities grow ever more expensive and the state too poor to help, the search is on for partners from the private sector. From sports to arts, in all walks of life, so why not death, the last walk, as well?
　Over the chapel: COOK'S TOURS OF THE HOLY LAND.
　The vicar SPONSORED BY PRUDENTIAL ASSURANCE.
　Inscribed on the coffin: WICKES DIY.
　Wreaths DONATED BY INTERFLORA.
　The hearse COURTESY OF HERTZ RENT A CAR.
　Undertaker's men DRESSED BY MOSS BROS.
　Over the grave: WINKWORTH ESTATE AGENTS.
　Spades and shovels OFFERED BY DYAS.
　Banner on the crematorium chimney: FLY BY BA.
　For afterwards: SANDWICHES BY MARKS & SPENCER.
And then we can afford to die.

It is rubber that perishes. People just die. Rubber is less common than people. It has to be nurtured. It possesses many important qualities, and is unselfish and accommodating. It lives chastely and is inoffensive and tidy in its perishing. Dying is what people do.

❧

IN one's age, aggravated by illnesses, the world shrinks and dissolves into the self; and the self is an impoverished thing, a set of symptoms, a memorandum of pills and prohibitions, a solipsist with barely an *ipse* to boast of. Every now and then, the soul remembers its Yeats, and does its best to clap its hands softly and sing a bit.
　Push aside the Sunday supplements and the latest fictions. You haven't the strength for them. Take up Dickens, say, so invigorating on both the individual self and the great world. Ottilie's splendid aphorism comes to mind (ah, one still has a mind!): 'You cannot give the

world the slip more certainly than through art, and you cannot bind yourself to it more certainly than through art.'

You present the GP's letter. Horrors! You are not on the hospital's computer. You have spent nervous hours and confused days there, yet they do not know you. The clerk shakes her head sadly. Then a thought strikes you: the GP is prone to misspell you as 'Enwright', a common Saxon solecism. You try again. Ah yes, the clerk smiles. You exist.

The Urology Clinic is awash with little bottles, bashful or brazen. Some people—mostly men, there's an occasional woman, ill at ease, as though she's incurred some shameful male disease—have brought theirs with them, old mustard pots, plastic pill boxes, herbal jars, turmeric, oregano, thyme. Others have not; they must extemporize. They see a large notice on the wall by the WC: 'One in three men over 50 has difficulty passing water. Do you?' Do I, they ask themselves. Suddenly they do. We have been waiting long, and some of us have no difficulty at all, and queue restively outside the WC. The Clinic is littered with little bottles. They pass from hand to hand. They are left perched on tables and ledges and miscellaneous machines. I recognize mine, it is a deep russet.

The valley of the shadow of death, through which the NHS conducts us with wandering steps and slow, seems interminable. We are sorry, we are too many.

Someone I know had a nephrectomy when he was a good twelve years younger than I am now. It was done privately. They told him it would be six months before he was back to normal. I was told it would take three months. The rich are different from us; they are more delicate.

One bad thing about ill health is that it makes you a hypochondriac.

'Feel like a piece of drawn threadwork, or an undeveloped negative, or a jellyfish on stilts, or a sloppy tadpole, or a weevil in a nut, or a spitchcocked eel. In other words and in short—ill . . . Before I went to sleep last night, my watch stopped—I at once observed the cessation of its tick and wondered if it were an omen. I was genuinely surprised to find myself still ticking when I awoke this morning. A moment ago a hearse passed down the street': W. N. P. Barbellion.

'What's the matter with you?'
'An ontalgia.'
'A what?'
'An ontalgia.'
'What's that?'
'An existential illness; it's like asthma but more distinguished': after Raymond Queneau.

'Favour': to spare, treat with tenderness. We favour a gammy leg, some other limb, this bodily part or that. There comes a time when favouring costs too much in disfavouring. Then death turns up and favours all.

My father couldn't pronounce 'chimney', it always came out 'chimley'; the contiguity of 'm' and 'n' was too much for him. I find I can't pronounce 'cystoscopy', it comes out 'cystocopy'; two 's's so close are too much for me. Chimlies have gone, cystocopies have come.

Part of hospital journal is printed in *Times Literary Supplement*. People tell me they find it very funny. True, I was scared into my wits.*

---

* See *Collected Poems 1948–1998*, pp. 503–8.

THERE are good, decent, kind people in the world. We all have the honour of knowing some of them. (We rarely *hear* much about them.) Yet a sickening miasma of awfulness hangs over us, a sense of de-civilization, of humanity rotting under the erosion of old inhibitions and compunctions, practically (so we thought) instincts. No point in drawing up a charge-sheet; it wouldn't be enough, and it would be too much.

What might the proportions be? A thousand good people conscious of the more or less dreadful acts of ten other people? (It's difficult to preserve unconsciousness.) Ten good people aware of the heinous acts of a thousand others? How long can those thousand or those ten survive, over how many generations, against the growing triumph of that genial rogue, or that demonic spirit, licensed—we were told—to allure, provoke, and energize us lazy beings into creativity?

Can it be that these things, 'what man has made of man', are much the same, *mutatis mutandis*, as they always were; and now, when so much more is reported, we know more about them, and inevitably most of what we know is evil or sad? (Folk wisdom does its best to console.) Or do fears of this kind stem from the quickening disintegration of one's own small ego, aggravated it may be by the recognition of one's own misdoings and derelictions? Is it all no more than the despair—self-spawned and invalid—of the world which precedes and possibly eases one's leaving it? Not, the end is nigh; merely one's personal end. But can one argue with one's strongest feelings like this? (It appears one can.)

Questions, questions. Do we really want to learn the answers? Let's hope—it's always on the cards—that one is simply off one's head. That way one has a better chance of staying sane. And of dying in one's 'right mind'.

Sheep and goats . . . Long-lasting bliss is hard for us to imagine. One theory had it that souls in heaven achieved it by observing the sufferings of the damned in hell. An early anticipation of soap operas on television. I dare say it would be rather pleasing to watch the well-deserved torments of certain individuals, for thirty minutes or so, with maybe a commercial break extolling the virtues of virtue. But throughout eternity? It sounds like hell. The good ought to be able to find better things to do.

My mother, who saw only good in others, used to warn me: 'Don't expect too much of people.'

※

DAINTY devices and edifying instances.

In his early twenties, crossed in love, Coleridge ran away from Cambridge and joined the 15th Light Dragoons, stationed in Reading. He enrolled as Silas Tomken Cumberbatch or Comberbache, a name spotted on a brass plate in Lincoln's Inn, and proved a hopeless soldier. When the men's carbines were inspected, the officer called out, 'Whose rusty gun is this?' Trooper Cumberbatch: 'Is it *very* rusty, sir?' 'Yes, it *is*.' 'Then, sir, it must be mine.' The manner of confession tickled the officer, and the trooper was spared. He was less lucky with horses, forever falling off one side or the other and bruising himself. (He seems to have stayed in place long enough to acquire boils on his bottom.) He bribed a young soldier to rub down his unruly steed by writing love verses for the youth to send his sweetheart. In the regiment Cumberbatch was considered an amiable idiot.

One day, as he was on sentinel duty, two officers walked past, chatting about Euripides; one of them quoted a couple of lines. Begging their honours' pardon, the sentinel corrected the Greek and observed that the lines actually came from Sophocles. The astonished officers had him transferred to the regimental hospital as an orderly. He was a great success with the patients, who declared that he did them more good than all the doctors. When he told them about the Peloponnesian War and how it lasted for twenty-seven years, 'There must have been famous promotion there,' one poor crock proposed. And another, more dead than alive, asked, 'Can you tell, Silas, how many rose from the ranks?' They had animated discussions, on the nature of the rations in those days, as to whether the famous general, Alexander the Great, could be one of the Cornish Alexanders, and whether the wide Hellespont wasn't the mouth of the Thames, which was very wide indeed.

Before long his friends secured the trooper's discharge by means of a sweetener of around £25 and on a technical doubt concerning his sanity.

Did the Romantics achieve their characteristic effects through an ability to remain 'in uncertainties, mysteries, doubts, without any irritable reaching after fact and reason'? (Perhaps most poetic effects are gained thus, disconcerting though it must be to those of us who worry over fact and reason.) Keats added that Coleridge would forgo 'a fine isolated verisimilitude caught from the Penetralium of mystery' by being 'incapable of remaining content with half-knowledge'. Yet in his *Table Talk* Coleridge records, approvingly, a clergyman's reply to a youth who said he would believe nothing he couldn't understand: 'Then, young man, your creed will be the shortest of any man's I know.'

Coleridge also relates that his father, when announcing the text of a sermon, would inform the congregation, 'That I may give you this injunction in the most solemn manner, hear the very words uttered by the Spirit of God', and then thunder out the Hebrew original. 'It did more good than all the rest of his sermon. The clowns in the gallery put their necks out and opened their mouths and were evidently impressed with something of a sense of the grand and holy.'

In one of his poems, 'On Ice', Erich Fried tells a story from his childhood. Arriving late at school, a boy blames the black ice on the roads: for every step forward, he had slipped two steps back. The teacher, nobody's fool, asks how in that case he had managed to get to school at all. Easy, said the boy: he had given up trying and decided to return home.

John Thelwall thought it very unfair to prejudice a child's mind by inculcating opinions before it had come to years of discretion and was able to take in fact and reason and choose for itself. Coleridge showed Thelwall his garden, whereupon Thelwall remarked that it was covered in nothing but weeds. Coleridge replied, 'That is only because it has not yet come to its age of discretion and choice. The weeds, you see, have taken the liberty to grow, and I thought it unfair in me to prejudice the soil towards roses or strawberries.'

In 1806, during a nocturnal storm, it occurred to Coleridge that it would be ideal to die by lightning. 'Death without pain, without degrees, without the possibility of cowardly wishes, or recreant changes of resolve. Death without deformity, or assassin-like self-disorganization. Death, in which the mind by its own wish might seem to have caused its own purpose to be performed, as instantaneously and by an instrument almost as spiritual as the wish itself.'

Indeed it sounds ideal, so persuasively does the poet represent the process. Except that wishing won't call down lightning. How many nights spent in wandering around and getting soaked to the skin, if not mugged, and wishing one were back in one's warm, dry bed? Electric chairs are not available on hire, and (besides a niggling doubt about that absence of pain and degrees) have the wrong associations. There must be a better way. One wishes one knew it.

In 1984 a resident of Perth, Australia, drank a cocktail of poisons, including fly spray, and swallowed 156 painkillers. This merely made him feel unwell. Distracted by no recreant change of resolve, he turned on a gas bottle, and lost consciousness. Waking up resentfully some hours later, he sought consolation in a cigarette. The resulting explosion blew the house apart and him through the door. He was unhurt, but found guilty of criminal negligence.

Ad lib

The actor's miming met with admiring murmurs,
until it became plain that he had forgotten his lines,
and—this was in Dublin—couldn't make out the promptings
of the prompter.
                              At last he drew himself erect.
'Many of you present are merchants, and know the value
of money. I have lost a thousand pounds—all I had—
lent to a friend . . . Many of you present are fathers,
and know the value of sons. My son, my only son,
lies dead on the battlefield. I have just received
the news.' With a handkerchief held to his eyes, he
tottered off the stage. Actions spoke louder than words,
and now the applause was clamorous and protracted.

A gentleman remarked: 'I have never heard of any son.'
Another: 'Neither did he ever have a thousand pounds.'
A third: 'His genius springs from the bottom of a glass.'
It was a lame translation of a limp German tragedy,
and the actor had transformed the evening for them.
'Let's treat the old rogue to another bottle.'

The peak point in *Wilhelm Meister's Apprenticeship*. Wilhelm and the beautiful Countess fall into an impulsive, ardent, and utterly unsuitable embrace. As she tears herself away, the Countess shrieks: 'Fly, if you love me!' It emerges much later that during the embrace a jewelled locket containing a portrait of her husband pierced the Countess's breast. Subsequently she became unshakeably though wrongly convinced that cancer had set in, and she turned to religion.

Hidden hereabouts, no doubt, are parables, any number of them. One day we must dig into them, reaching determinedly after fact and reason. One bright summer's day, when we are in better shape.

※

CARRYING a stick in the Underground does sometimes get you a seat. As long as both you and the stick are clearly visible. Don't expect too much of the grim-faced young woman engrossed in her paperback, *A Guide to the Advanced Soul*. The other day an Indian gentleman offered me his standing room. How affecting such gestures are. I could have kissed his hands.

After an examination, you are recovering from the anaesthetic. Where are your shoes? Do shoes always go astray in hospital? A plump black nurse, her name is Gladys, says, 'Silly boy, they're under the bed, in the proper place.' She's 'not very well qualified'; she presents you with a cup of tea and a chocolate biscuit. They are delicious.

You are seeing someone who turns out to be the senior registrar about the results of a biopsy. He leafs swiftly through a fat file, your curriculum mortis. Perhaps he's going to let you know the number of your days. No, he lets you know, somewhat inexpectantly, his views on smoking. He says he saw you just before you had your operation last year. He was about to go on holiday, he remarks with a smile. For a whole year, you are tempted to ask. You don't remember him. 'Oh yes, of course,' you say with a smile.

A nurse remembers you from a year ago. You are so pleased. You remember her of course, vividly, but since then she has seen hundreds of patients, barely distinguishable one from another. You ask what became of the man in the bed opposite yours—Frank Stagg, you made friends with him—he was still there when you left the ward, you gave him your phone number. Her face stiffens, she mumbles that she's sorry, she doesn't remember. Perhaps she does remember.

It seemed the rules had changed. You could use a word only once, and then it disappeared. As if it had died on you. The words you wanted were the commonest ones, and you soon used them up. Then there was only silence. Nothing you could do about it, or anyone else. There were faces. You stared silently into them, they stared silently into you. They were looking down, you were looking up.

You wake in a sweat. That was a chilling dream! Something to do with language, you suppose, something you had been reading, about words fading out. (You had thought they lasted for ever.) Just their fading out, you hope.

'Too old a dog to learn new tricks,' you tell yourself complacently. Adding with muted pride, 'Always was.' Oh no you weren't. When you were (within bounds) a young dog, you learnt new tricks as best you could. You had to, to get where (such as it is) you are today. They were, you well knew, tricks, not always congenial, but necessary, indeed essential, and somehow you had let yourself in for them. By now they have acquired the authority of self-evident laws. Laws which younger generations of dogs, puppies you'd call them, ignore at their peril. You can't believe they'll ever grow to be old dogs.

I am ticked off for excessive and indiscriminate swearing. I have devalued the whole treasury of imprecations. Montaigne mentions the Thracians who, during thunderstorms, would shoot arrows into the sky with the intention of getting back at God and bringing him to his senses; and also the philosopher Bion, asking of a king who was tearing his hair out, whether he thought alopecia relieved grief.

The most telling instance of impotent rage, old age's forcible-feeble, comes from Lear. 'I will do such things,/What they are, yet I know not, but they shall be/The terrors of the earth.' Lear is on the brink of tears, 'women's weapons, water-drops'. This utterance—you can hear the anguished hesitations—brings me close to weeping, another indiscriminate excess of age.

A different sort of impotence, this time in respect of loving requital, in George Herbert's 'The Thanksgiving': 'Then for thy passion—I will do for that—/Alas, my God, I know not what.'

What happened to the critic in you? Watching a wholly undistinguished drama on television, and at the end, when the badly injured little girl is seen fit and happy, your eyes are on the verge of filling. Literary criticism must be for the young and hardy.

'*Tolle lege*,' a small voice is saying. 'Come on!' So I take up the Bible and open it at random. 'And when the children of Ammon saw that they stank . . .' Yes, I suppose it's time I had a bath. But that's from Samuel; and Augustine, I seem to remember, relied on Paul. So I open the book again, towards the end, and read: 'Even so we speak; not as pleasing man, but God, which trieth our hearts.' It would. Thanks, but I'll settle for a bath.

> *Decadent dirge*
>
> *Dec*ade, I would say—
> De*cade*'s 'disputed' still, though
> Less and less each year.

HEARING unexpectedly that a friend is unconscious and near death. Sadness, rather stultifying, obscurely aggrieved. Then being told that he is sitting up and reading. (It wouldn't be anything trivial.) Deep relief... Though you guess it can be no more than a respite. (What more than a respite does one ever look for?) At least it gives you time, a chance to bestir yourself, to sit up and run through memories, perhaps run through one or two of his books. As if his revived consciousness has revived yours.

The pessimist says, The more people you know, the more to lose. True. The optimist says, The more people you know, the more to keep. Very true. But why is it the pessimist always comes out on top?

When I bump into him next I must ask what he thinks of this new book. He's very good on the subject. But I can't—he died last year.

'Jesus have mercy': the last thing I heard my old friend mumble, in a moment of bleak lucidity. I try to recall that eloquent voice ringing through the lecture hall.

Norman MacCaig dies. Most amenable of poets, delivering a new collection of exactly the right size every second year. In Herbert's terms, he rested in Nature decidedly more than in the God of Nature. (Not, as such things go, a major misdemeanour.) Empathetic in outlook, or inlook, even solipsistic, but with nothing of the Egotistical Sublime; rather, something of the altruistical ridiculous.

'I am, too, a centre/of roundabouts and No Entries, libraries,/ streets full of cafés, and the prickly stink/of burnt petrol'; 'I clack my own beak/by my own burrow/to feel how many little fishes/I've whiskered home'; 'Shall I call myself Earwig/and trek manfully on, seeking/the crumb of comfort?' Quite sublimely ridiculous.

Not hard to envisage MacCaig's heaven: a large, fetchingly cluttered place, and plenty of time to explore it.

George Mackay Brown: a smooth, easy transition—he was never much of a traveller—from one Orkney to another.

When Gavin Ewart arrived at the gates, they would surely have handed him a halo of laurel—the kindliest of men and (what's more) of poets, he never bit a back. Yet certain of his poems must have been impounded and quietly taken away for burning. Perhaps not, though; we know so little about the current climate of opinion in those parts. It could be that the poems were photocopied and circulated among the souls who on earth had endured the multiform sorrows of 'sec or secs or whatever they call it'.

Time to call a halt. A request to reprint something written ages ago arrives from Gale Research Inc., Detroit, addressed to my literary estate.

Index

Aaronovitch, David 9
Adorno, Theodor 128–9, 171–3
Ai Qing 155, 159–61
Ajax 16
Alain 39–40, 126, 154
Alexander the Great 21, 192
Ali, Muhammad 14
Althusser, Louis 86
Amiel, Henri-Frédéric xvii, 19, 57, 65, 67, 179
Amis, Kingsley 34, 124
Amis, Martin 25
Andrews, James Pettit 48–9
Archimedes 6
Aristophanes 164
Aristotle 86
Aspel, Michael 76
Auden, W. H. 121
Augustine, St 197
Austen, Jane 87

Bach, J. S. 47
Bagehot, Walter 163
Bainbridge, Beryl 110
Barbellion, W. N. P. 189
Barnes, Djuna 71
Barnes, Julian 36
Barthes, Roland 60, 112
Bataille, Georges 51
Baudelaire, Charles 104, 114, 126
Baudrillard, Jean 48
Benjamin, Walter 168
Bennett, Alan 62–3, 178
Berryman, John 98
Bierce, Ambrose 12, 34
Binchy, Maeve 63
Bion 197
Blake, William 66, 70, 102, 127
Bloom, Harold 67
Blunden, Edmund 135
Bogarde, Dirk 28

Boilly, Louis 173
Böll, Heinrich 77–8
Borges, Jorge Luis 19, 21
Botton, Alain de 97, 145
Bowie, Malcolm 38
Bradbury, Malcolm 23
Bragg, Melvyn 37
Brecht, Bertolt 68
Britten, Benjamin 110
Brodsky, Joseph 104
Brookner, Anita 131
Brown, George Mackay 199
Buchan, Charlotte 9–10
Buchan, Claire 8
Buchan, James 150
Buchan, Jamie 8–9
Burchfield, R. W. 185
Burgess, Anthony 94
Bussy, Dorothy 73
Burke, Séan 111–12
Butler, Hubert 57
Butler, Samuel 121

Calvino, Italo 128, 156–7
Campbell, Thomas 33
Cantona, Eric 14–15
Caroline (wife of George II), Queen 24, 49
Carroll, Lewis 177–8
Castaneda, Carlos 138
Celan, Paul 61
Chang Jung 8
Chao Tai 143
Chekhov, Anton 116
Cicero, Marcus Tullius 48
Cioffi, Frank 151
Cioran, E. M. 45–8
Cixous, Hélène 71
Clarke, Arthur C. 123
Clausewitz, Karl von 104
Cleary, Jon 140

201

Cleland, John 95
Cockman, Thomas 48
Cockton, Henry 94
Coleridge, Samuel Taylor 51, 53, 103, 167, 191–2, 193
Colette, Sidonie Gabrielle 3
Collins, Joan 32–3
Conan Doyle, Sir Arthur 176
Confucius 59, 81, 113
Connolly, Cyril 154
Conquest, Robert 23
Conrad, Joseph 74
Currie, Edwina 65

Dagg, Mr 24–5
Dalby, David 137
David (Book of Psalms) 140
Davies, Robertson 94
Delanty, Greg 106
De Quincey, Thomas 165–6
Derrida, Jacques 51, 67, 111
Descartes, René 79
Dexter, Colin 18
Diana, Princess of Wales 177
Dickens, Charles 56, 60, 150, 151, 157, 175, 176, 187
Dickinson, Emily 112–13
Diogenes 125
Domecq, Adèle, 54
Donne, John 80–2
Drake, Sir Francis 120
Durcan, Paul 129
Durrell, Lawrence 113

Eckermann, Johann Peter 54
Eco, Umberto 66–7
Edward VII 74
Eliot, George 60, 95, 135, 164
Eliot, T. S. 9, 129, 135–7
Elizabeth I 120
Elizabeth, Princess (daughter of James I) 82
Ellis, Alice Thomas 7
Ellis, David 86
Emerson, Ralph Waldo 44, 79, 158
Empson, William 23, 162

Enright, George 23, 189
Enright, Grace 170, 191
Enright, Madeleine 8–9, 77, 139, 165–6, 178, 181–2
Epicurus 149
Eribon, Didier 52
Euripides 191
Ewart, Gavin 199

Faraday, Ann 168
Fauré, Gabriel 57
Feng Yuxiang 7
Fielding, Henry 25, 56
Fish, Stanley 67
Foucault, Michel 52–3, 70
Frederick, Elector Palatine 82
Freud, Sigmund 86, 151, 180
Fried, Erich 192–3
Friedan, Betty 139
Fullerton, Mary 122
Furbank, P. N. 63

Gaarder, Jostein 115
Garth, Samuel 60
Gascoigne, Paul 14
Gauguin, Paul 116
Gide, André 73
Goethe, Johann Wolfgang von 18, 54, 70, 103, 117–18, 125, 137, 141, 142, 143, 145, 146, 164, 187–8, 194
Goldwyn, Samuel 2
Golffing, Francis xvii
Gorky, Maxim 57
Gowrie, Gray, Lord 26
Greene, Graham 135
Greville, Fulke 179

Hackett, Sir John 28–9
Hale, Terry 145
Hall, Willis 119
Halliwell, Kenneth 101
Hardy, Thomas 66, 119, 127
Hawthorne, Nathaniel 17
Hawtree, Christopher 36
Haycraft, Colin 68
Heaney, Seamus 126

Heidegger, Martin 51
Heine, Heinrich 40, 84–5, 106
Helps, Sir Arthur 56
Herbert, George 11–13, 14, 57, 138, 197, 198
Hobhouse, John Cam 139
Holden, Grace 28
Hölderlin, Friedrich 92
Holmes, Richard 24–5
Honecker, Erich 164
Housman, A. E. 171

Jacobson, Dan 1–2
James, Henry 17
James, P. D. 28
James, William 18
Jesus 15, 21, 81, 82, 119, 132, 153, 154, 166
Job (Book of) 47
John Paul II, Pope 164
Johnson, Samuel 25, 34, 60, 66, 76
Josipovici, Gabriel 2–3
Joyce, James 3, 16, 70
Judas 21
Juvenal xvii, 68

Kafka, Franz 42–5, 60, 91
Kant, Immanuel 84–5
Kawabata Yasunari 184–5
Keats, John 103, 170, 192
Kempe, Margery 82–3
Kermode, Frank 23
Kierkegaard, Søren 30, 125, 157–8, 175
Kilmartin, Terence 143, 144
Kirkham, Sir Graham 76
Knox, R. A. 89
Kraus, Karl 3, 23, 69, 132, 172

Lacan, Jacques 67, 86, 87
Lao-tzu 167
Larkin, Philip 23, 150
Lawrence, D. H. 157
Leavis, F. R. 16, 19, 95, 100, 163, 178
Leopardi, Giacomo 55
Levin, Bernard 101
Lewis, Jeremy 48

Leys, Simon *see* Ryckmans, Pierre
Lotringer, Sylvère 51
Luke, David 118
Luke, St 153
Luther, Martin 81, 165

MacCaig, Norman 198
Macherey, Pierre 86
Machiavelli, Niccolò 164
MacKillop, Ian 16
McNair, Major 75
Madan, Geoffrey 89
Madonna (Madonna Louise Veronica Ciccone) 65
Mailer, Norman 14
Maintenon, Mme de 49
Mallarmé, Stéphane 35
Mann, Thomas 15, 22, 47, 163, 164, 176
Mantegna, Andrea 166
Mantel, Hilary 16
Mao Zedong 8
Maradona, Diego 14
Mark, St 154
Matthew, St 49, 154
May, Derwent 36
Mazarin, Jules 117
Melville, Herman 131
Ménage, Gilles 48, 49
Mencken, H. L. 131
Michelet, Jules 3
Miles, Jack 56, 145
Miller, Henry 3
Miller, Karl 63
Milosz, Czeslaw 9, 85, 104
Milton, John 16, 79, 87, 102, 111, 120
Montaigne, Michel de xvii, 7, 68, 81–2, 114, 196–7
Moore, George 78
More, Kenneth 28
Motion, Andrew 177
Mozart, Wolfgang Amadeus 14
Murdoch, Iris 63, 175
Murray, John G. (Jock) 95
Musil, Robert 14–15, 20, 176

Nabokov, Vladimir 17, 139
Nicholas, Ted 105–6
Nietzsche, Friedrich 4, 6, 47–8, 51, 96, 105, 162–4

O'Brien, Conor Cruise 129
Onwhyn, J. 94
Orleans, Duchess of 49
Ortega y Gasset, José 142
Orton, Joe 101
Orwell, George 136

Paglia, Camille 70
Pascal, Blaise 2, 46, 106
Paul, St (I Epistle to the Thessalonians) 197
Pelé (Edson Arantes do Nascimento) 14
Petronius 164
Pilate, Pontius 170
Porter, Peter 141
Powell, Anthony 129, 150
Proust, Marcel 93, 97, 113, 143–5, 176, 180–1
Puccini, Giacomo 130
Putnam, Hilary and Ruth 18

Queneau, Raymond 189
Quine, W. V. 170–1

Raffles, Sir Thomas Stamford 147
Richardson, Samuel 27, 113
Ridley, H. N. 75
Rifkind, Malcolm 165
Rilke, Rainer Maria 98, 99
Rimbaud, Arthur 14
Robinson, Henry Crabb 145
Rochester, John Wilmot, Earl of 121
Rohmer, Sax 171
Rossetti, Christina 93
Rushdie, Salman 39–40, 116
Ruskin, John 51, 54, 96, 166
Russell, Lilian 71
Rutherford, Mark 40
Ryckmans, Pierre (Simon Leys) 6, 59, 113

Sade, Marquis de 9, 60
Samuel (2 Book of) 197
Sartre, Jean-Paul 135
Savage, Richard 24–5
Schiller, Friedrich 25
Schmidt, Michael 20
Schopenhauer, Arthur 162–3, 169
Scott, Paul 143
Scott, Sir Walter 113
Scott Moncrieff, C. K. 143, 144
Scupham, Peter 121
Shakespeare, William 2, 18, 47, 59, 68, 69–70, 81, 86, 87, 110, 117, 131, 135, 168, 197
Shattuck, Roger 9, 112, 123
Shaw, George Bernard 30
Shelley, Mary 22
Shelley, Percy Bysshe 99, 163, 175, 182
Simenon, Georges 127
Sisson, C. H. 105, 175
Smallwood, Norah 28
Smith, Sydney 94–5
Socrates 21
Solomon (Book of Proverbs) 12, 154, 158, 186
Sommer, Piotr 176–7
Sophocles 191
Spencer, Charles, Earl 177
Steiner, George 83, 142, 163
Stern, J. P. 42, 43, 60
Strachey, Lytton 64, 73
Svevo, Italo 58

Tanner, Michael 45, 47
Tasso, Torquato 55
Thelwall, John 193
Thomas, R. S. 180
Thornton, Arnold 62
Trevor-Roper, Hugh 36
Trollope, Anthony 87
Trollope, Joanna 185
Tsvetaeva, Marina 104

Unseld, Siegfried 91–2
Updike, John 14

Valéry, Paul 104, 129
Victoria, Queen 56, 139
Virgil 21
Voltaire 86

Wagner, Richard 101
Walden, George 26
Walser, Robert 91–2
Warner, Sylvia Townsend 20
Webster, John 17
Whittle, Sir Frank 64
Wilbur, Richard 137

Wilde, Oscar 33, 117
Wilkins, John 154–5
Winter, Helmut 146
Wise, Ernie 164
Wollstonecraft, Mary 70, 71
Wordsworth, William 135
Wright, Jemmy 89
Wyndham, John 123

Yeats, W. B. 61, 187

Zhou Enlai 160